interviewing

Gail Sedorkin

2ND EDITION

interviewing

A guide for journalists
and writers

ALLEN&UNWIN

This edition published in 2011
First published in 2002

The author acknowledges the contribution of Judy McGregor to the first edition of this book, some of which has been retained or adapted in this new edition.

Allen & Unwin
83 Alexander Street
Crows Nest NSW 2065
Australia
Phone: (61 2) 8425 0100
Fax: (61 2) 9906 2218
Email: info@allenandunwin.com
Web: www.allenandunwin.com

Cataloguing-in-Publication details are available
from the National Library of Australia
www.trove.nla.gov.au

ISBN 978 1 74237 094 1

Set in 10.5/13 pt Garamond by Midland Typesetters, Australia
Printed in Australia by McPherson's Printing Group

10 9 8 7 6 5 4 3 2 1

For Lisa

CONTENTS

Acknowledgements   vii
Introduction   viii
  1 The interview   1
  2 Research   32
  3 Getting started   55
  4 Breaking the ice   73
  5 The questions   83
  6 Print interviews   108
  7 Broadcast interviews   125
  8 Telephone and email interviews   153
  9 Using the information   164
 10 Keeping safe   179
Resources   194
List of personal and email interviews   200
Index   201

ACKNOWLEDGEMENTS

My first thanks must go to my sister Lisa, who contributed to the content of this edition, and also researched, proofed, supported and encouraged me, together with my husband Nick, my mother and father, Mollie and Lou Svanetti, brother Andrew and sister-in-law Ada. The support and encouragement of friends and colleagues Barbara Alysen and Mandy Oakham was also invaluable.

For their time and expertise I would like to thank Ian Baker, Janie Barton, Peter Bennetts, Craig Borrow, Andrea Carson, Channel 7, Peter Davis, Jon Faine, Liz Gray, John Hamilton, Beth Harvey, the *Herald Sun*, Sharon Hill, Dorothy Horsfield, Louise Keller, the late Paul Lyneham, Jodie Munro O'Brien, Network Nine, Kerry O'Brien, Robert Reid, SBS Publicity and Andrew Urban.

And, of course, at Allen & Unwin, Elizabeth Weiss, who kept the project going, and Jo Lyons for her meticulous editing, attention to detail, patience and support.

Gail Sedorkin

INTRODUCTION

Almost every journalist has a horror story or two to tell about their first interviewing attempts—failing to ask questions, not listening to the answers, having a recording with no sound, or returning to the newsroom practically empty-handed are common disasters.

David Leser says that his first interview twenty-two years ago, when he was working for *The Daily Telegraph* as a cadet journalist, is still etched in his brain.

> It was my first day on the job and there was an industrial dispute and I had to call management and workers to get a response. This was my very first call for my very first story and I was so nervous that, when the person answered the phone, I promptly forgot not only whom I was calling but why I was calling (2001: 8).

Cadets' interview training often consisted of watching a senior reporter for a few days before being let loose to sink or swim, despite the fact that interviewing is an integral part of journalism and professional writing. In fact, Ken Metzler believes that 'good reporting is about 80 per cent interviewing', and goes on to ask, 'What is the point of being a good writer if you have nothing of substance to convey through your writing?' (1977: 133).

Bob Jervis agrees that 'interviewing is the most important, and the most difficult, skill of the journalist'. It takes the 'average cadet . . . about eight weeks to become a reasonably adept intro-writer; about a year to learn to structure a fairly complicated news story passably; and much, much longer to become a competent interviewer' (1989: 96).

There's no more daunting prospect than having to meet with a total stranger for the sole purpose of eliciting information from them on a topic you know little to nothing about. Interviewing ranks on the stress levels right up there with giving a one-hour speech to a crowded room but, as with giving a speech, there are three keys to success:

1 preparation
2 preparation, and
3 preparation.

Masterton and Patching sum it up in just one line: 'In every case the best interviews are those that are best prepared, with the best questions in the best sequence, and where the reporter listens carefully to every word of every answer' (1997: 202).

This is the main point I am making in this book, and it is stressed again and again in the tips, checklists and advice provided by some of the best interviewers from around the world. Cadets, trainees and students were also canvassed about their major fears, and I hope that they will find answers to their questions in these pages.

Organise your contact book (which will quickly become your bible), let my research tips guide your own digging, adapt my questions to your topic and incorporate my step-by-step guide to each and every interview you conduct. Following the best practice guidelines in this book will allow any writer to craft superior stories from quality interviews.

To make the most of your interviews, however, enjoy the incredible opportunity you have to talk to so many interesting people!

REFERENCES

Jervis, B. 1989, *News Sense*, Advertiser Newspapers Limited, Adelaide, SA

Leser, D. 2001, 'The interview: art or a confidence trick?' *The Walkley Magazine*, issue 13, p. 8

Masterton, M. and Patching, R. 1997, *Now the News in Detail*, Deakin University Press, Geelong, Vic

Metzler, K. 1977, *Creative Interviewing: The Writer's Guide to Gathering Information by Asking Questions*, Prentice-Hall, New Jersey, USA

THE INTERVIEW

Karl Stefanovic:	Are you a monster?
Anne Hamilton-Byrne:	I'm not conscious of what you're saying, I should be conscious of.
Karl Stefanovic:	Are you a monster?
Anne Hamilton-Byrne:	Certainly not.
Karl Stefanovic:	Are you evil?
Anne Hamilton-Byrne:	Well, what do you call evil?
Karl Stefanovic:	The systematic abuse of children is evil.
Anne Hamilton-Byrne:	No.

(Excerpt from *60 Minutes*, Channel 9 2009)

If the purpose of this exchange was dramatic television then it could certainly be seen as a successful interview. If, however, the aim was, as for most journalistic interviews, to illicit 'information and insights' (Brady 2004: 1), very little was achieved in this clash. The interview was conducted by Karl Stefanovic for *60 Minutes*, questioning alleged cult leader and child abuser Anne Hamilton-Byrne.

Today interviews, particularly those broadcast on television, can attract very large audiences. But what is an interview? Is it a conversation between two people or an exchange in which one person challenges the other, a way of tricking people into revealing facts or an argument in which two opponents are pitted against each other? Is it an opportunity for the interviewee to give a speech, or is a journalist merely a conduit for channelling information from the source to the public? It could easily be argued that interviewing is all of these, and more.

Journalism educator and publishing consultant Professor John Brady states that interviewing is 'a little bit like going on a blind date. It's basically a process of getting to know someone by asking questions and getting answers. In many ways, this is something we've been doing all our lives, and it is usually a very comfortable process.' (Brady 2004: 1).

Today an interview can be anything from a rapid exchange to get a small 'grab' or 'sound bite' (an answer or part of an answer that can be as short as one second for broadcast), to a lengthy feature interview in which the whole exchange—questions and answers—are published or broadcast.

Bashir: Did your relationship go beyond a close friendship?
Diana: Yes it did, yes.
Bashir: Were you unfaithful?
Diana: Yes, I adored him. Yes, I was in love with him. But I was very let down. (PBS 1995).

The two questions and dramatic answers—above—came from one of the most talked-about media interviews of our times. The one-hour interview with the late Diana, Princess of Wales, and BBC1's Martin Bashir broadcast in November 1995 was viewed by millions of people around the world. The *Panorama* interview was promoted as one in which Princess Diana 'talked openly about her life, her children, her failed marriage, her eating disorders and depression, her husband's relationship with Camilla Parker-Bowles and her own infidelity' (PBS 1995).

A popular definition of interviewing is that it is a conversation with a purpose—to inform, entertain and challenge audiences. The interview is the main way in which journalists collect information for news stories. The better the interview, the better the information and the stronger the story. Interviewing is an integral skill for the journalist and one that is difficult to master.

All interviews are different. They may involve trying to elicit opinion or emotion, or just gathering fact. Author of *The Electronic Reporter* Barbara Alysen makes a distinction whereby 'the *tone* of the interview will also vary, from hard, to soft, to emotional ... Reporters are also called upon to conduct *emotional* interviews such as those with the victims of crime or accidents, or their relatives' (Alysen 2000: 130; original emphasis).

Mainstream news media rely on fact and opinion interviewing, and magazine journalism uses human interest interviewing for soft news and feature pieces. On the other hand, newer media formats are rewriting traditional definitions to respond to technology and changes in public taste and consumer patterns.

Fact and opinion interviews relate more to hard news, while the human interest interview is used for soft news or feature pieces. The *fact* interview usually concentrates on the Who, What, When and Where questions, and is used for print news briefs and broadcast news stories where space and time are limited. The interview for *opinion* or *comment* emphasises the Why and How questions, and is more commonly used in longer stories. As Masterton and Patching note: 'A journalist wit is supposed to have said that while the broadcast news reporter chases fire engines, the current affairs reporter is down at the fire station talking to the fire chief about how to improve the service' (Masterton and Patching 1997: 239). The *human interest* interview also includes *fact* and *opinion* questions, but concentrates on the emotions and the soft news angle (as in the interview with Princess Diana).

The *Compact Oxford English Dictionary of Current English* defines the interview as 'an occasion on which a journalist or broadcaster puts a series of questions to a person of public interest', with its French form *entrevue* derived from *s'entrevoir*, 'see each other' (Soanes and Hawker 2008). However, not many interviews are conducted *s'entrevoir*—face-to-face—today. Tighter deadlines and generally smaller newsrooms have resulted in fewer of these 'meetings'.

Journalists, particularly electronic journalists, are increasingly reliant on telephone interviews, media conferences, doorstop interviews (where you catch someone as they are leaving another appointment), as well as email and satellite interviews. Skype is also rapidly becoming a very popular interview method, with the exchange frequently broadcast for immediate use. This immediacy was demonstrated in the Haiti earthquake reports on Wednesday 13 January 2010, delivered by Haitian radio and television presenter Carel Pedre, which is covered later in the book. One of the few sources of information for journalists, Pedre was linked with Skype interviews shortly after the disaster, while journalists on site faced difficulties broadcasting using satellite technology with no sources of power—except batteries of abandoned cars (according to news reports at the time).

TYPES OF INTERVIEWS

Vox pops

Vox pops (*vox populi*: voice of the people) are used regularly by print and broadcast journalists and have the benefit of immediacy and spontaneity. Essentially they are street surveys to canvass people's feelings about a person's actions or a topical issue. For instance, numerous vox pops have been conducted on smoking in public and on the popularity of political leaders. The question should be short, easily understood and 'open' (that is, the question should elicit more than a yes/no response). Everyone who is interviewed should be asked the same question to ensure the validity of the results.

Doorstops and ambushes

There are some drawbacks to spontaneity, and the doorstop method is one that should be used with great care to gain an interview. A doorstop interview in which the interviewee is asked to respond to accusations or allegations of serious mis-behaviour is usually an adversarial situation. The interviewee can be inexperienced and at a disadvantage when appearing on television.

Doorstops are now used regularly—but not always as an aggressive technique. It is sometimes the easiest way for jour-nalists to catch busy sources when they are on their way to or from an appointment. For instance, you may catch a politician after a media conference or a celebrity leaving a concert or launch. Television journalists regularly use this technique, and in fact may doorstop an interviewee as they leave another media interview. Often doorstop interviews will be prear-ranged. Catching celebrities at airports or on the red carpet at premieres is now very common.

Deathknocks

Deathknocks are interviews in which the journalist knocks on the door of relatives and friends of someone who has just died to talk to them about the deceased for a story. Print and electronic journalists are expected to do deathknocks, which can be a difficult part of the job, particularly for cadets. Sharon Hill, editorial staff manager at Nationwide News, says their reporters are trained to conduct deathknocks politely and carefully:'The fact is our journalists are very rarely turned away. People actually do want to talk about their loved one, and a story in the paper—so long as it is accurate and positive—is a great comfort to them.' She has developed a number of hints to deal with this sort of interview. They include:

- Put your notebook and pen in your back pocket. It's threatening to open a door and see a stranger with pen and notebook poised.
- Always introduce yourself.
- Check details with the family as information from the police can be wrong.
- Use open body language and try to behave as any other professional who comes into contact with a family when someone has died suddenly. The police, the ambulance, solicitors and funeral directors are all part of the process, and so, often, are journalists (personal interview with Sharon Hill).

Sometimes a deathknock is not always a bad experience, as in the case of the interview with *A Current Affair* host Tracy Grimshaw with a young Cowra policewoman, Shelly Walsh. On telling her story of the murder of her children and her mother by her father, Walsh said after the interview that it was 'life-changing for her. It was very cathartic for her to tell it' (Grimshaw in Reinhold 2009: 21).

Senior police reporter Jodie Munro O'Brien says the deathknock would have to be the worst interview for a journalist because of the sensitivity of the situation. 'I don't know any reporter who likes intruding on a family who has just lost a loved one, in order to write a story. These, along with some court stories, are among the interviews you are most likely to be verbally abused at' (personal email interview with Jodie Munro O'Brien).

Jodie recounted her first deathknock as a young journalist in America, published by the Dart Center for Journalism and Trauma, University of Washington, together with a helpful guide, as a resource to help journalists who cover violence. An excerpt appears below.

It was late July 2000. As I drove the 45 minutes to the small country town, all I could think was 'please don't let them cry in front of me'. I was a young journalist and I was off on my own to interview the family—a mother specifically— of 12-year-old Billy Huddleston whose murdered body was found only the night before. No one taught us how to handle such a situation ... Many thoughts went through my head as I drove—how do I approach the grieving family? ...In this case, fortunately, the family was willing to talk because, at this point, their son's murderer had not yet been caught nor even identified ... I did not, at first, pick up my notebook. I offered my condolences ...I expressed that I did not know what they were going through, that I could only imagine, how it was unfair. I said it gently, compassionately, delicately. I apologised for being there at all and for having to meet under these circumstances. I offered them thanks for being courageous enough to talk to the media about the situation ...I took it slow. (Munro O'Brien 2007).

Years after this first big traumatic news report in North Carolina Jodie and her husband returned to Australia to live, where she is now the senior police reporter for *The Courier-Mail* in Brisbane. She is still occasionally in touch with Billy's mother.

Rounds and events

The work of the journalist can be roughly divided into three main 'beats' or events, which include: general or daily rounds;

managed events; and spontaneous or on-the-spot events. These all involve different interview contexts.

General rounds involve interviewing sources such as police, fire and ambulance services several times a day—usually by telephone. This round is often given to cadets, or less experienced reporters, and while it might seem tedious it can result in some of the best stories and leads. Please do not be discouraging in your questioning like the cadet who used to ask: 'You don't have any news for me, do you?' Not all rounds are daily. For instance, in Far North Queensland one round involves annually calling the local wildlife park to find out if the crocodiles are nesting (a sign that the wet season is on the way).

Managed events include media conferences and launches and are a common source of information for journalists today. The managed event is ideal for the organisers, giving them the opportunity to disseminate information to a large number of people at one time—a 'group interview'. One of the few advantages for the journalist is the chance to ask questions of a person who ordinarily would be impossible to catch on a one-to-one basis. The journalist can also use the answers to other journalists' questions in their story.

However, this definitely was not the case with the press conference held by golfer Tiger Woods on 20 February 2010, viewed by millions around the world. While he apologised for his behaviour and his many affairs with a prepared statement, no questions were allowed, much to the frustration of journalists. Golf commentator Frank Nobilo of New Zealand says he was displeased by the absence of a question segment. As Nobilo points out, the questions don't have to be about the number of women he had affairs with or who they were (Both 2010: 110).

On the other hand, there is no opportunity for an individual reporter to get a scoop, or an exclusive, when they ask their questions in public at a media conference. The organisers might allow individual time at the end for journalists, but generally it is a matter of trying to conduct a doorstop as they leave if you want to ask a question solely for your own benefit.

Spontaneous events can include anything from allegations of corruption to disasters and accidents. They offer the most interesting interviews and often supply the best stories, but are generally the most difficult situations for journalists because of the lack of preparation time.

INTERVIEW STYLES

Kerry O'Brien. (Courtesy of the Australian Broadcasting Corporation)

Journalists use different styles or approaches (genres). These can range from the aggressive interviewer who argues with the interviewee at every point to the interviewer who is overawed by the 'talent', agreeing with every word and allowing the interviewee to remain unchallenged.

> I'll adopt an adversarial approach and from one day to the next and from one hour to the next I may argue opposite points of view. If you interview the man from the bank on the day of the tellers' strike, I might put to him all the union's arguments, and then five minutes later I might be interviewing the union rep and I'll put to him all the employers'

arguments. What I'm doing is I'm trying to test their points of view. And in order to put their point of view to the test I have to understand the opposite point of view and be able to follow it up (personal interview with Jon Faine).

Other styles include the conversation and the challenge. Highly respected Australian political journalist Kerry O'Brien, who won the top award in Australian journalism, the Walkley, in 2000, uses the challenge style for most of his interviews. The following segment was taken from a television interview he conducted on 15 May 2000 on the ABC's current affairs program *The 7.30 Report* with International Olympic Committee (IOC) vice-president Kevan Gosper. Gosper had been publicly accused of nepotism for allowing his daughter Sophie to be the first Australian to run with the Olympic torch in Greece. After a brief introduction Kerry does not waste any time getting to the point with his first question.

Kerry O'Brien: Kevan Gosper, you've acknowledged an error of judgement, how serious an error?

Kevan Gosper, IOC Vice-President: It's serious for me, because I allowed my personal feelings towards my daughter and I guess in my Olympic heart, to make a wrong call and I regret that and I've tried to express my apology as sincerely as I can ...

Kerry O'Brien: I have to ask—why did it take so long for you to realise the error of judgement?

...

Kerry O'Brien: Did it occur to you that the Greeks might have been currying favour with you as a very powerful individual inside the IOC ... given the problems that they're having in preparing for the 2004 Olympics?

Kevan Gosper: The fact is it never entered my mind.

...

Kerry O'Brien: It sounds like you're still not absolutely convinced it was the wrong thing, rather than it's wrong because of the way it was perceived. Isn't it true, though, that the only reason Sophie was invited—given that privilege—is because you were her father? (ABC TV 2000).

THE SOURCES

Journalists must be adept at a number of skills to conduct an interview. While others can help with writing the story, you're generally on your own for the interview. Journalists must decide how the interviewee is feeling about the interview and match their style accordingly. If the interviewee is looking apprehensive, the reporter might not start the interview with the toughest question. Journalists often modify their approach according to their 'talent'. For instance, they would not use the same interviewing style in an exchange with a politician as they would when interviewing a young sportsperson.

Bell and van Leeuwen agree that the media interview can take on many forms, including where 'interviewers talk to politicians in the voice of the interpellator; to experts in the voice of the student; to ordinary people in the voice of the social researcher or the counsellor; to children in the voice of the parent or teacher; to "deviant" interviewees in the voice of the interrogator' (1994: 22). Not only are there different interview types and styles, the subject of the interview has a critical effect on its outcome.

For this reason it is common for broadcast journalists to use a limited number of sources that they know are 'good talent' because they have proven to be articulate and concise. These sources are often called 'talking heads' or, as Barbara Alysen describes them in *The Electronic Reporter*, 'the usual suspects'. She says 'the result is that the same speakers are seen and heard again and again. It becomes boring and it's unrepresentative'

(2000: 144). A journalist's range of contacts should be broadened by asking current sources for names of anyone else who could be interviewed on the same subject.

Politicians and CEOs

These interviewees are placed together in a category, as they use the media regularly to get their message out and are generally the most adept at handling interviews. Political and business leaders are eager to take advantage of any free space or air time. They are generally well versed in how to manage the media and deal with tough interviews, and often use public relations people as conduits. Before challenging any of these people in an interview, it is crucial to be armed with all the facts and to have researched what's been said before. Reporters need to be willing to persist and insist on answers to crucial questions. A skilled interviewer will overcome avoidance and evasion of tough questions.

Celebrities and sports stars

Celebrities, such as movie, music and sports stars, have something to sell and need the media to do so. However, they can also be quite overwhelming to the novice interviewer. A useful technique to overcome this 'awe' is to always use their first name—in other words, be familiar. Celebrities have been interviewed frequently and are often bored with the process, so it is important to develop some original questions.

The innocents

There are many interviewees who unwittingly become the focus of the media, or must participate in interviews because of their position, their actions or the actions of others that affect them. Generally journalists can distinguish people who are 'sources for the moment' and modify their approach accordingly. For example, obviously a journalist would approach survivors of a train crash with more sensitivity than a hardened criminal who has been sentenced for committing a major crime.

Criminals

It is important to be as objective as possible when interviewing criminals—showing neither empathy nor condemnation. This can be very difficult in cases that involve an interviewee who has committed a heinous crime. Journalists must distance themselves when approaching these interviewees.

Children

Young people are perhaps the most difficult to interview—particularly on air. Common ground should be established before the interview goes live. This could include asking about school, sports, movies or hobbies. Codes of ethics or statements of principles guiding journalists and broadcasters generally refer to the way in which reporters should deal with children in sensitive interviews. Caregivers' permission to conduct the interview is usually required when children are sixteen years of age or under.

Experts

Australian freelance journalist Peter Davis knows that interviewing experts can be a real challenge—especially when their expertise is way out of your own field. He's found a simple way to overcome these difficulties.

I once had to interview a whole lot of physicists about cold fusion technology. They may as well have been speaking Swahili for all I knew. But I asked each one of them the same question: 'How would you explain that to someone who has never studied physics?' Without exception, they all came up with some wonderful quotes that even I could understand (personal interview with Peter Davis).

TOP TECHNIQUES

Whether for hard or soft news, managed or spontaneous events, you must be interested in your interviewee—and show it. The best techniques for handling interviews from some of the best interviewers have been included here.

Preparation

Kerry O'Brien believes whether you're just starting out in journalism or whether you've been in the game for 30 years, preparation is enormously important.

The more you know about the topic, the issue, or the person—the better off you are. I don't have any particular tricks in the way I do interviews, I simply endeavour to understand as much as I can by way of background reading on the subject. I try to focus in on its essential elements. What are the things that the public would really want to know about this? Which are the most interesting and compelling aspects? The more ignorant you are about either the person or the issues, the more it will show up—it's very hard to hide that. You'll often find that busy people, important people, people with pressures on their lives and on their time, will get very impatient very quickly if they feel you're stuffing them around and you don't really know what you're on about. But regardless of what their attitude is to you, you should at least have respect enough for your readers, or your audience, to do as much preparation as you can to understand the topic in advance (personal interview with Kerry O'Brien).

Eye contact

The top tip from Australian print and broadcast journalist Andrew Urban involves the use of body language and, more specifically, 'eye contact'.

> My eyes don't move. I don't get easily distracted, even when we're talking on the street with cars going past, people jumping around behind the person I'm talking to, and children crying. I focus solely on the subject. I constantly listen for any clue while trying to work out the next question. It can be very difficult and very draining—but it works (personal interview with Andrew Urban).

Atmosphere

Journalists usually try to create a comfortable atmosphere for the interviewee—even if they have to destroy it later in the interview by asking the tough question. Andrew Urban believes that what journalists want most from an interview is a revelation given only to them, and that there are a number of ways to ensure that this 'revelation' occurs.

> I want to make sure people are comfortable, are not threatened. I am not confrontational—I believe the honey gets the ants. I think it's the approach—a lot of information is given in the start of the interview. Journalists should be sceptical—not cynical. If you're cynical you've limited what you're going to get—you need the luxury of being objective. I convey the feeling that it's fine, it's okay, I have no imperative and this makes them comfortable. It is merely the opportunity to have a conversation (personal interview with Andrew Urban).

Concentration and listening

Well-known Australian radio journalist Jon Faine believes there are three essentials for every interview: preparation, concentration and listening. Listening is often described as a neglected skill, but its importance in interviewing cannot be overstated.

> The key to whether I make a good job or a bad job of the day's interviews is whether I'm concentrating ... And if you stop listening to your guest's answers you'll miss things and you won't ask the most obvious thing which the audience are all shouting at you to ask as they're driving in the car, or in the kitchen doing the baking, and they say 'how could you not ask that next question?' (personal interview with Jon Faine).

Described as one of the 'legends of television', Sir Michael Parkinson has interviewed more than 3000 of the world's 'movers and shakers' including politicians and entertainers. When asked by Channel 7's David Koch for his secret to good interviewing he said, 'It's a simple proposition, really . . . you listen and then you follow up. The secret is listening' (Channel 7 2009). However, even this 'secret' did not help the ill-fated interview with actor Meg Ryan, who unexpectedly did not make 'good talent'.

Parkinson decided he would start the interview with Ryan using questions 'to settle her' (or icebreakers), which in effect seemed to do the exact opposite. It would seem she wasn't expecting to answer questions relating to the previous two guests, British fashion experts Trinny and Susannah. When Ryan did speak to the girls it was to say, 'Oh, did you just do a fashion item?' (Parkinson 2008: 205). Parkinson states that he 'knew in that moment [he] was not going to make friends with Meg' (Parkinson 2008: 205).

In fact, Parkinson reaches a point during the interview where he decides it is better to conclude the discussion, as the only thing he feels he could ask is why would she come to the interview and then not make any effort to participate. Parkinson then 'told her she obviously didn't like being interviewed, that her demeanour and body language suggested she wanted no part of our show and, that being the case and she having been a journalist, if she was in my shoes, what would she do? "Wrap it up," she said, which was the only sensible quote I got from her all night' (Parkinson 2008: 205).

Silence

It is commonly agreed that silence can be a useful technique in interviewing. Sometimes used as an aggressive technique, journalists believe that if they wait long enough the interviewee will feel obliged to fill the space. However, this can be difficult for radio journalists, who will be left with what is known as 'dead air'. In some interviews, though, if the journalist wants 'considered' answers they should be prepared to wait.

Respect and curiosity

Kerry O'Brien believes respect and curiosity are the most important 'natural assets' for interviewing. 'I think a respect for people is actually vital—curiosity about people, yes, but an understanding of a human being's basic right to a sense of dignity' (quoted in Wilson 2000: 95). He believes curiosity is one of the fundamentals that drives journalism.

> Let your curiosity flow. God knows where the expression curiosity killed the cat came from. Even when you're in a live situation and you're thinking 'I really want to ask this question but it's going to sound silly'. In most cases you should go ahead and ask it anyway. If it's a question that's

driven by your natural curiosity, then there's every likelihood that other people would want to hear the answer too (personal interview with Kerry O'Brien).

Andrew Urban believes the interview is like a small love affair. 'It's like falling in love a little bit at an intellectual level. And you know it happens when there is a sudden falling away of barriers, and they decide to trust you with their information' (personal interview with Andrew Urban).

Andrew is well known for his ability to make people open up about their private lives—people he has never met before. How does he do it? He has three golden rules:

1 Never judge people.
2 Never make fun of people or manipulate them; never create a freak show.
3 Always make them the centre of attention.

TECHNOLOGY

Technology has increased the number of ways in which an interview is now conducted. Email, satellite and now Skype interviews are used more frequently and are ideal tools for the journalist trying to contact people outside their time zone. While extremely useful for a journalist with limited time—and an interviewee with even less—these interview forms have their drawbacks.

While most of the non-verbal clues are missed with a telephone interview, the tone of voice can be gauged, and instant feedback helps prompt new questions. Email interviews lack spontaneity, allowing the interviewee time to consider and edit their answers with no direct pressure to answer the actual questions. Satellite and Skype interviews have the advantage of allowing a 'real time' interview even when the two (or more) parties are not in the same city, state or country. However, not all satellite interviews have return vision (whereby both parties are able to see each other). The interviewee might be talking directly to a camera in another studio and might not be able to see the journalist—so again there might be a lack of non-verbal interaction. Skype interviews can also mean contending with calls that drop out and inconsistent sound quality when compared to mobile or landline phones.

Face-to-face interviews are preferable for journalists because they yield so much more information than the other methods. Not only are the answers articulated on the spot, but also the body language of the interviewee can give clues for further questions and confirm the validity of the answers. Sometimes the non-verbal clues are more revealing than the verbal answers. It is a discouraging sign if a celebrity frowns after being asked about their private life. However, if they are leaning forward and smiling, it could be seen as a signal that they are happy to continue. Having the guest in the studio rather than interviewing on the telephone guarantees a better level of interaction between the guests and interviewer.

It guarantees that the body language can come into play . . . You will always get your story told better if you agree to a studio interview, and some people insist on that. So we much prefer them, but it's just not physically possible within the constraints that many of our guests have on their working days, to come in and give us the time we would like to get from them (personal interview with Jon Faine).

Telephone and email interviews are covered in detail in Chapter 8.

WAR ZONES

This photograph of journalist Jodie Munro O'Brien was taken at an Iraqi vehicle checkpoint in between the towns of Tallil and An Nasiriyah in southern Iraq. An Iraqi police officer is in the background.

Jodie Munro O'Brien is a senior police reporter for *The Courier-Mail* in Brisbane, Queensland. She completed a Bachelor of Arts and an honours degree in journalism at Central Queensland University, Rockhampton—which she swears was only a couple of years ago. Jodie started her full-time career as a journalist halfway through her honours degree at a local weekly newspaper in the same city in mid-1997. A few months earlier, she was one of two honours students chosen to participate in a month-long internship at *The Jakarta Post* in Indonesia.

Jodie moved to the United States in September 1998, where she first worked on the copy desk of a daily newspaper in western Pennsylvania. After about a year there, Jodie and her American husband, Tom, moved to Charlotte, North Carolina.

Now able to remember to stay on the right side of the road when driving in the US, she worked as the city council reporter and then the chief police reporter at a daily newspaper called the *Independent Tribune* outside Charlotte while also freelancing for a magazine owned by *The Charlotte Observer*. A couple of years later they moved to Asheville, North Carolina, in the midst of the Blue Ridge and Great Smoky Mountains, where she worked as the night police reporter for a daily newspaper called the *Asheville Citizen-Times* and freelanced on the side for an outdoors magazine.

Despite loving the mountains, Jodie (originally from Mareeba in tropical Far North Queensland) was tired of cold, snowy winters. The promise of more scuba-diving and warmer weather called to Jodie and Tom and they eventually moved to central Florida, outside Orlando, in September 2003. Jodie worked for the *Daily Commercial* newspaper—in one of the most media-competitive parts of Florida—first covering government before returning to her passion, being the chief police and court reporter.

Over the years Jodie has enjoyed a couple of stints as acting chief-of-staff, was lucky enough to pick up a couple of journalism awards along the way, covered too many murdered children stories, and remains amazed that Tom is always understanding of her receiving phone calls for breaking news in the middle of many nights or on weekends.

Jodie, Tom and their blue heeler, Sydney (she has an American bark), all moved to Brisbane in May 2006. Jodie worked for *The Gold Coast Sun* as the city council reporter and then as the education reporter for *The Gold Coast Bulletin* (Gold Coast Publications) for about nine months, adding a border collie named Boston to their troupe along the way.

Jodie moved to *The Courier-Mail* in 2007, where she worked as a senior police reporter. The following year Jodie travelled to Iraq, where she worked as a journalist and photographer for the major daily newspaper. Jodie and Tom now have their daughter, Leia, as the latest addition to their family.

'Anyway, back safe'

Though a police reporter, Jodie spent two weeks in Iraq in April 2008, writing—and taking photographs—about the Australian Army being pulled out by the then prime minister, John Howard, in June 2008. The following is an account of some of her experiences in Iraq. Despite some close calls, Jodie hopes to return soon.

Although News Limited has a full-time defence reporter based in Canberra, there are occasional opportunities for other journalists to take trips to cover certain stories such as I did with going to Iraq.

About a year later, another *Courier-Mail* journalist from our features department had the opportunity to go to Afghanistan for a couple of weeks. So as you can see, any journalist could potentially end up being sent into a war zone or other dangerous zone (hurricane, earthquake, etc.) at any time in their career.

On the trip to Iraq in 2008, we spent most of our time in Tallil in southern Iraq, although we also travelled with the other journalists to Baghdad for a few days. It was an exhausting two weeks and we were so busy that I never even got to finish writing all of the potential stories I came across. I filed the more pressing ones from Iraq and continued working on and writing any subsequent stories on my return to the *Courier-Mail*'s newsroom.

In my case I had to take my own photographs because the military said there was only limited space for the media so they could not fit one more person—in this case our photographer. They told me an Australian Army photographer would be available for us, but I didn't count on that happening so I actually took my own camera. As it turns out, that was the best thing to do because the army photographer was not with us much and did not leave the base or come out on patrol with us at all while we were there. If a key news story had broken while we were on patrol I would not have had photos of any breaking news—or any photos at all for that matter—to go with the stories I did write.

I would definitely recommend having a camera with you at all times if possible. In our short trip's case (about two weeks including international flight time; in country was only about 1.5 weeks) we had three television reporters but only one cameraman, who had to be the pool cameraman for Channels 7, 10 and the ABC. Plus, the pool cameraman did ABC Radio sound work too as the ABC journalist had to file for ABC TV, radio and online.

There were two daily newspaper journalists on the trip—myself and a reporter from the *Sydney Morning Herald*, plus another journalist from a military magazine. We were not allowed to photograph inside our flight or conduct any interviews with the soldiers onboard on the way over.

The media contingent was a challenge in itself on the trip to Iraq. Because of the TV stations, who need to obtain various different angles for their footage for their station alone (and times that by three TV stations in this case), us print journalists would be finished and ready to move on to the next stop or to write, but we were always having to wait for the electronic media to do their stand-ups, etc.

Unfortunately this made us run late for almost everything, which then cut our time short at other spots and also meant we didn't get to start writing or filing until quite late at night or, depending on the time we got in and our deadlines, had to get up incredibly early in the morning to type.

Our days generally started at 6.30 am anyway, so we'd have to get up and work prior to that or skip breakfast to get work done. In some cases, some of us did not go to sleep at all. As I had to file stories and photos, at one point I literally went two and a half days without sleeping.

I know the pool TV cameraman/radio sound was the same way. After three days of no sleep he opted to not come with us on one patrol because of pure exhaustion. Again, if something major had happened, that would have been a problem. The Channel 7 reporter at least brought his own small handheld camera so at least they would have had that, but he was not impressed that the pool cameraman was not with us.

Having said that, we appreciated everything we had on our schedule, and we all wanted to do everything on the schedule. It was perhaps a bit jam-packed considering our limited resources for visuals.

We had briefings to attend, usually led by officers, who gave us an overview of the area we were in, the purpose of the troops being there, and gave us a chance to ask questions. Although these were very important for us to attend for key background information with good quotes, these were not the entire story. Our Public Affairs Officer (PAO) escort or officers would often choose, organise or recommend a certain soldier for us to interview.

We were always under escort (also because of safety reasons; we were in a war zone, after all). The Australian Army accommodated us very well. Of course, I am sure most of those we interviewed were media trained first. However, I was also able to chat to others of lower ranks at other times who may not have been through the training, which was my preference. Usually we were given officer after officer, but we wanted to speak to the majority—the lower ranked troops on the ground as well.

I personally took advantage of any opportunity to talk to privates who were not necessarily handpicked to chat to us. For example, there was an occasion where we were on patrol in the middle of the night in an ASLAV (Australian Light Armed Vehicle) and we were delayed for a couple of hours. While our PAO and the other media sat in the back in the dark and tried to get a bit of sleep (sitting up), I got put on the headphones and chatted with the two privates who were the drivers of the ASLAV. This proved to be beneficial in a couple of ways—I got to know the 'truth' about how some of the soldiers felt; I found out about another potential story; and I made some army contacts. This also proved useful a few months later when another story broke out back in Brisbane and those contacts were able to provide some information to me confidentially.

Overall, we were fortunate in that on this trip we were given a lot of opportunity to get certain stories and if we asked our PAO if we could interview someone else he tried his best to arrange it.

We mainly dealt with the Australian Army although we often ran into some US Army and, of course, we all ate in the American Dining Facility Administration Centre (DFAC) with the Americans, Aussies, British and Romanians. Because they were expecting us, the Australian Army was very accommodating. I find it's mostly when we are back in our own country that the bureaucracy takes over and makes things difficult. Our Australian Army PAO told us not to take photos of certain things or landmarks, even though we saw American soldiers taking photos of those same items, which was a bit frustrating. Most of these types of photos would have only been for our own personal souvenir use anyway—like damaged bunkers on base in Kuwait from the 1990s war with Iraq. But we complied with the PAO's request as we wanted to use common sense and to ensure if there was ever another opportunity to return, we would be welcomed by the army.

The PAO also wanted to screen our photos before we sent them back to our newsroom. However, he said this was only to make sure nothing classified was accidentally photographed in the background—and we all had common sense, so he found nothing of note from any of us anyway. I, personally, didn't have a problem with this, as I was certainly not there to jeopardise anyone's mission or safety! I don't believe any of the other media had a problem with this either.

The Army PAO didn't scan our copy though, although he did watch the TV reports before they were filed. I don't know if he did that to check the vision (again for items in the background that they did not want photographed) or if he was just interested in what was going to be aired. Either way, he never read my stories or the *Sydney Morning Herald*'s before we filed them. The only thing that hindered my stories was, again, the above jam-packed/running behind schedule thing with the TV stations. Once we were in Iraq, we came across other potential stories. However, we did not have much time to follow them up, which was very frustrating when we wanted to get all the stories we could and do the best job we could.

This was also because we were supposed to be escorted everywhere, so if there were not two escorts available at the time, print journalists could not go one way while the TV reporters went the other. This left me (and others) with stories still to write on our return to Australia. I actually had to call back over to Iraq from my office in Brisbane to do some interviews they didn't have time for me to squeeze in while there because of that. At my paper, this also seemed to hinder the chance of getting those stories published—the more I could file direct from Iraq, the more chance I had of getting them published.

We were mostly in southern Iraq at the Tallil Air Base though they did manage to squeeze in a quick tourist stop for us to the Ziggurat of Ur. This was awesome. Our trip was mainly because our Aussie troops in southern Iraq were being withdrawn in June 2008. It would have been great to spend more time in Tallil as we were not able to walk around as much—I probably would have also done a bit of a human interest story or feature here about the Ziggurat, given the chance and time.

We were also close to the city of An Nasiriyah—the scene of a March 2003 battle where US soldiers and Marines were killed. Although we went on a patrol on the outskirts, we did not have the chance to go into the city. The day we arrived in Kuwait the Australian Army CO [commanding officer] had actually gone into An Nasiriyah to meet with some leaders. He told us if we had been there then, he would have taken us! This would have been an excellent story—to have a western CO talking to the leaders of such a town—however, we arrived after the fact. All of these types of suggestions were later relayed back to the Australian Army—who sought feedback on the trip—in the hope that any future media trips with the army could be planned even better. I highly recommend taking the time to send feedback to organisations such as the military for trips like the one to Iraq, as not only does it help make any potential future trips more successful, but it helps establish even better contacts.

Towards the end of the visit to Iraq, we flew to Baghdad for two days—though really only 1.5 days were of any use. We were going to be taken in a Rhino Runner [an armoured bus used extensively in Iraq] into the International Green Zone (IZ) in downtown Baghdad one day to meet with the Australian ambassador at the embassy and another official. Unfortunately for us, a dust storm picked up about thirty minutes after we landed in Baghdad and the military mostly does not fly when there's a dust storm. Because of the dust storm, they predicted—correctly—that the insurgents would be firing overnight in the IZ because the dust acts as a blanket. As a result of this dust storm, we found out in the morning when we were supposed to be heading out to the IZ that we were no longer allowed to go.

We all protested this, saying we knew the risks of where we were, otherwise we would not be there. However, of course it was for our safety. Our problem here was this day was our only chance to go to downtown Baghdad, and we very much wanted to go there—that would have been one of our best stories, we think. For trips into major cities or areas like this, having a bit more of a chance to go again if it is cancelled would have been helpful.

The next morning (the day we left to return to Kuwait), we were informed that an American was killed at the very spot we would have been at about the time we would have been there!

In Tallil they gave us our own room with Internet access

for filing stories and photos. We all had our own laptops. Although I had a program to use to get into my newspaper's story filing program (called Cyber Express), I found it easier to just email the stories back to my editor. The Internet service was often slow and sometimes down in Tallil. However, we managed. The television crew used a satellite line. I also FTP'd [used File Tranfer Protocol to send] photos back but, again, I needed the Internet for that.

In Baghdad, they set us up in the Aussie soldiers' welfare room, where there were some computers and phones. The soldiers were informed we would be in there for a couple of days but, of course, they were still allowed to use the room. This didn't affect us in any way, as again, we had our own laptops so generally stayed off the desktops that were in there.

We were set up with a special log-in from the military, in both Tallil and Baghdad. We did need access to phones in both spots, which we generally shared with each other. Most of the time soldiers in Baghdad would be on the phone at a different time or wouldn't be long anyway, because of the time difference. We were not allowed to use our mobile phones because of potential bugging.

We did run into a problem in Baghdad one night— when the dust storm and the firing and bombing started downtown. It was late at night and the phone lines were all knocked out. Those of us who were still up working just kept typing in a Word document and crossed our fingers we would be able to file, or at least read, our stories over the phone. Luckily, they had IT employees working 24 hours a day so they managed to find a way, eventually, to hook us up to somewhere else, but it did take a couple of hours.

Jodie's experiences, which she is keen to repeat, prompted some advice for all journalists.

Especially if you're at a bigger paper (or TV station), have a 'grab bag' ready to go and leave it either in your car, or in a locker or your desk at work. This should include toiletries and a few changes of clothes for different weather situations. Pack enough for at least two to three days. There is always a chance you could get sent somewhere for breaking news at a moment's notice—floods in the outback, a terrorist attack or other major news overseas. Often a plane will be booked for you and you may not have time to drive home to get a bag ready in time to get back to the airport.

REFERENCES

Alysen, B. 2000, *The Electronic Reporter*, Deakin University Press, Geelong, Vic

Australian Broadcasting Corporation (ABC) TV, 15 May 2000, 'Gosper cleared over Salt Lake City', *7.30 Report*, http://www.abc.net.au/7.30/stories/s126909.htm, accessed 4 March 2010

Bell, P. and van Leeuwen, T. 1994, *Media Interview—Confession, Contest, Conversation*, University of New South Wales Press, Sydney, NSW

Both, A. 21 February 2010, 'Tiger's "gone for the year"', *The Sunday Mail*, p. 110

Brady, J. 1 November 2004, 'Just asking', *The Writer*, vol. 117, no. 11, pp. 28–31, http://www.writermag.com; Australia/New Zealand Reference Centre database, Accession no. 14728645, pp. 1–5, accessed 15 March 2010

Channel 9 2 October 2009, 'The Family', *60 Minutes*, story transcript, http://sixtyminutes.ninemsn.com.au/stories/870619/, accessed 22 January 2010

Channel 7 15 July 2009, Michael Parkinson interview with David Koch, *Sunrise*, Sydney, NSW

Masterton, M. and Patching, R. 1997, *Now the News in Detail*, Deakin University Press, Geelong, Vic

Munro O'Brien, J. 2007, 'Encountering Traumatic News for the First Time', *Australasian Update*, newsletter, Summer, http://dartcenter.org/, accessed 22 March 2010

Parkinson, M. 2008, *Parky: My Autobiography*, Hodder & Stoughton, London, UK

Paul, I. 14 January 2010, 'Tech tools tell the story of earthquake in Haiti', *PCWorld*, pp. 1–5, http://www.pcworld.idg.com.au/article/332380, accessed 21 January 2010

Public Broadcasting Service (PBS) 1995, 'The Princess and the press: Diana's 1995 BBC interview', *Frontline*, interview transcript, WGBH Educational Foundation, 1995–2010, Boston, http://www.pbs.org/, accessed 3 March 2010

Reinhold, L. 21 December 2009, 'The story that broke my heart', *Woman's Day*, p. 21

Soanes, C. and Hawker, S. (eds) 2008, *Compact Oxford English Dictionary of Current English*, 3rd edn, revised, Oxford University Press, Oxford, UK

Wilson, R. 2000, *A Big Ask: Interviews with Interviewers*, New Holland Publishers, Sydney, NSW

2 RESEARCH

Celebrity, actor and television host, Ernie Dingo.

The interview with popular television personality and actor Ernie Dingo, at the time of the release of a new television program, *Outback Wildlife Rescue*, was to be conducted by phone. Dingo has been interviewed by hundreds, possibly thousands, of journalists so it was essential to find a different angle, a different way to tackle the interview. With little time for research the Internet proved most useful with background information on Ernie Dingo, the new program he was hosting and several biographies. One of these from the Channel 7 site revealed that Ernie Dingo was an ambassador for the Fred Hollows Foundation. This information begged the question: why, of all the charities he could support, did Ernie Dingo devote his time to the foundation? The answer was revealing and produced the following angle for his story.

'A grasshopper loose in Queensland,' sang the young boy with a huge grin on his face. 'As big as any goose and he drinks pineapple juice all over Queensland,' he continued singing to the older man. The boy was a very young Ernie Dingo singing one of his favourite Slim Dusty tunes to eye doctor and surgeon Fred Hollows, as he worked, checking the eyes of all the children of Ernie's Western Australian community, Mullewa (extract from 'Ernie's Choice', Sedorkin 2008).

What use is research? Why should research be undertaken before an interview, and what happens when you don't have enough time? Certainly in this case it meant a new angle and hopefully a more interesting interview for the celebrity.

The national deputy news editor for Special Broadcasting Service (SBS) Radio, Sally Spalding, believes that if you don't do your research, then you're not doing your job properly.

You have to do your research to do your job well, and to do justice to your job, and to do a good interview you're going to need that information. You can do an average job, or a mediocre job, but you won't get the best answers (personal interview with Sally Spalding).

WHY RESEARCH?

Here are eight main reasons why research is useful.

1   Research helps you establish credibility as a reporter. It takes a certain amount of courage to ask questions, particularly if you have never met the interviewee before. Those you interview will be more inclined to talk to reporters

who have done their homework and gathered background information.

2 Research improves your confidence in asking 'hard' questions. Knowing that you have a document up your sleeve or quotes or comments from someone else, or information from another source to reinforce the question you have asked, gives you the courage to press for answers. Tough or embarrassing questions often have to be asked, which could provoke a hostile reaction. Doing your homework means there is less chance of having your ignorance exposed.

3 Research enables you to get more out of an interviewee. You can go in and try to wing it just by using the five W's and one H (Who, What, When, Where, Why and How), but often you need a lot more than that.

4 Research allows you to know when someone you are interviewing is avoiding the question or evading the truth. Journalists and tax collectors have something in common: they learn to recognise the infinite ways interviewees can fudge facts in difficult situations. Fact-fudging could be the result of acts of omission when information is withheld, acts of commission when lies are told, unintentional misleadings and deliberate red herrings. Increasingly, too, reporters covering areas such as politics or commerce have to pierce the shield of public relations practitioners who are guarding their clients. A recognition of the pitfalls and shortfalls of spin-doctoring is possible if you have done your homework.

5 Research helps you understand trends, patterns and relationships. Some of the best stories written come from reporters who not only have an eye for spot news, but also can see an 'issues' story developing. From their experience, from talking to sources, from reading and from looking back over their clippings and listening to their audio and visual recordings they recognise social, political or economic

trends. Whether your particular round is health, education, local politics or crime, you should be able to write or script topical backgrounders by keeping abreast of unfolding developments.

6 Research helps you keep an upbeat pace during an on-air or live broadcast interview. Kim Hill, Radio New Zealand's *Nine to Noon* interviewer, says, 'The more research you do, the faster on your feet you are. I think that's the main object of an interview, to be fast on your feet. Otherwise the interview gets bogged down, and you get stuck on one issue. You need to know enough about a subject to volley . . .' (Hill 1996).

7 Research allows you to angle the news so that you are not repeating stories others have already broadcast or written. Chief reporters and news editors would doubtless cite as their greatest frustration the number of stories presented to them by reporters that do not refresh a running story with a new angle.

8 Research improves accuracy. It helps untangle incorrect information and verify facts, dates, names, numbers and what sources have said previously. Remember, you owe it to the people you interview to get it right. It has been said that the interview is a conversation with consequences. The celebrities, the politicians, the officials, the sports-people, the eyewitnesses and the ordinary people in the street who are interviewed by journalists are being judged not just by the reporter but also by everyone who reads, watches or hears their comments.

THE TIME FACTOR

Time is the enemy of good reporting. All reporters feel that in some interviews they haven't asked the right question or gained the most from a newsworthy person because their preparation time for the interview was limited. So what can you do when you have no time for detailed research? The pace of the newsroom means that few reporters have the luxury of research for every interview. They often hurtle to airports or meetings armed only with native cunning, a scrappy assignment note and recording device, camera crew or a notepad.

Most journalists are armed with a BlackBerry or iPhone these days with functions that include email, voice calls and Google Earth searches. In particular journalists are discovering Google Earth's usefulness for on-the-spot research, if only to find the location of an interviewee with its ability to bring up a view of a street address, house, building or landmark. Should a story break while out in the field, then it is possible to find the location without the cumbersome use of a directory or local street map. In addition to a search function Google Earth also includes a 'search near me' function, which for example will show where a business is located with no need to type in the name of the location. A recent entry into the mobile market is the Google Nexus One. It is the first mobile phone that has been produced by Google and also sports the feature Google Earth. In 2008 Google Earth was made available for the Apple iPhone by Google. It is now free and can be downloaded from the iTunes Applications Store (*Cell Phone Digest* 2008).

This might read like a testimonial for the Apple iPhone 3G S, but on the day of its release it actually played an integral part in creating a broadcasting breakthrough in the form of a newscast story that was televised by WFOR-TV (US digital channel). 'Even the Poynter Institute, a school and resource for journalists, mentioned the innovative use of the iPhone 3G S applications to create a story in their daily podcast about what in the media was making news that day' (Benitez 2009). I-Team Producer for CBS4, Gio Benitez, after lining up and purchasing the Apple iPhone 3G S at the Falls Shopping Centre, Miami, conducted interviews and took video shots of the customers while they were waiting in line. 'Oddly enough, not one of these Apple fans found it strange that a television station was shooting video with an iPhone!' (Benitez 2009).

Here are two research strategies—one short-term and one long-term—for discovering background information when you know little or nothing about the person whom you will be interviewing.

Short-term strategy: Ask naively dumb, but not completely stupid, questions

Most people you interview realise that journalists cannot be experts on every subject and every person. There are times when you have to be brave enough to ask naively dumb questions without appearing completely stupid. Coax the subject of the interview to explain the background of a conflict, dispute or issue so that your readers, listeners or viewers will understand. Asking technical experts to explain something complex in lay terms is another way of getting the story without revealing your ignorance. Another technique is to encourage eyewitnesses to tell their story in their own words first so that you can pick up enough to ask relevant follow-on questions. Never pretend to know more than you do. The humble journalist who flatters the interviewee and coaxes answers from them will come away with a better story than the reporter who feigns knowledge and writes in ignorance. Be honest enough to say you don't understand or don't know when it is appropriate so that interviewees provide the missing information.

Long-term strategy: Develop background knowledge to rely on

Curiosity killed the cat—but it sustains the journalist. Journalists are by nature, and by calling, inquisitive. To be professionally curious, though, reporters need to build their own banks of knowledge about the rounds they cover, their communities, politics and the issues of the day. The more information you store about a topic, the more curious you become about the unanswered questions and the unexplained doubts. This background knowledge can be the journalist's secret weapon, and it can form the basis of interview questions when you have had no direct time to research a specific interviewee.

Background knowledge is developed by:

- your own personal reading
- seeking out news and current affairs through watching television, listening to the radio and reading newspapers and magazines
- regular contact with your sources
- talking to other journalists in the newsroom, particularly the good reporters
- involving the librarian in your job so she or he alerts you to anything you might not see or hear
- thinking about your work.

When you have no time for formal research you will be more confident about asking the spontaneous question because you have invested in your own bank of background knowledge and current affairs information.

Sally Spalding of SBS Radio advocates the long-term strategy of developing background knowledge.

You have to make sure that you're on top of the topic by listening to the radio each day in the morning to the top stories ... You should also try to see at least one TV bulletin each night ... The best journalists that we've ever hired into our level one position (which is our entry level position)

. . . are the ones who always come in the door in the morning for an eight o'clock start and have read the papers at home before they get to work. They're the most impressive staff that we've had. And the ones that get to work and think, 'I'll read the papers when I get there', never hit the ground with their feet running, because you have to brief them before they go out on a story. Well, my expectation is that they know the story before they get here, not that we have to tell them what they should be asking and what the story's about (personal interview with Sally Spalding).

A generic rule of thumb is that a journalist should have read (not cover to cover) at least two newspapers and one radio bulletin before coming to work. Online news sites are helpful in that headlines and videos are available.

FINDING THE ANGLE

One news editor used visual aids to teach young reporters the value of an 'angle'. He would make the first folio of the hard copy of the story that was not up to standard into a paper dart. That was before he spiked it. This taught journalists in the newsroom to spend extra time finding an angle.

What angle is required, and what length should the story be? Is the story merely a reaction piece to splice into a longer story, or is it a full interview?

Research is essential to find the angle that no one else has. For example, the newsroom might have received an anonymous tip-off and wants you to put the information to someone, or radio might want follow-up reaction to a story that is already available online. But remember, don't just blindly follow newsroom advice. Act on your hunches too, and don't close your mind to new surprise angles in a story.

Before beginning the research ask yourself:

* How much do I know about the subject?
* What do I want to find out? (The litmus test for this might be to ask yourself what is it that the public wants to know.)
* Where can I find the information?
* What is the quickest way to retrieve it?

CLIPPINGS BOOKS AND COMPUTER FILES

Clippings books provide a speedy update on stories. The time-honoured tradition of cutting and pasting the stories you write for print media into scrapbooks is alive and well in most newsrooms. Referring to clippings books as a living resource means that you do not repeat old news or begin at the wrong start point.

Clippings books become part of your CV and can be used to show off your stories when applying for other newsroom jobs. Electronic filing is necessary and now news outlets have their own search engines that provide electronic updates and easy access to stories and photos using keyword searches and databases.

LIBRARIES

The best advice for a new reporter in the newsroom or at university is to immediately make friends with the librarian. Librarians are secret resources. They know where to get information and how to get information. They can save you from mistakes and alert you to story possibilities. In newsrooms where the reporter population is young and mobile, it is often the librarian who has the most historical knowledge of events and issues in the area. In some newsrooms the librarian attends daily news conferences and is given the assignment list to begin collecting information for the interviews of the day. Where there is no newsroom librarian, public library facilities offer similar but often less specific resources.

TIPS

1 Learn how to search electronically archived stories and photos.
2 Make a friend of your librarian—they can help make or break good interviews.

Media libraries have moved to electronic access, although in some newspaper libraries there is currently a combination of archival clippings and contemporary electronic filing. Past happenings, and even people, can be accessed via photographic file searches.

You may be located close to specialist libraries such as technical libraries, archives and university libraries. Whatever story you are researching there is likely to be a matching specialist library that general librarians can help you find.

The interview with Ernie Dingo (see p. 32) was conducted by phone, and the key to ensuring that specific details were accurate regarding quotes for a song 'Grasshopper: Loose in Queensland' was due to the use of research and a knowledge of sources to try. If you don't know the answer or where to look, always ask.

VIRTUAL LIBRARIES

A vital part of accurate research requires verifying the information or facts. Sometimes journalists or writers find that obvious sources such as their local library do not hold the information sought or it might not be directly accessible online. When this happens and a deadline is looming, a virtual reference service you can try is AskNow, a national chat service staffed by librarians throughout Australia and New Zealand from national and state libraries. Online resources in the form of an email transcript of a session including web links can be sent. Web pages can also be 'pushed' to clients, and the librarian can also co-browse the same screen with the client. The availability of this service depends on which state you are submitting your query from, so make sure you check first.

To access AskNow you can start at your national or state library's home page. Queensland State Library's home page has a quick link called 'Ask Us' at http://www.slq.qld.gov.au/. This quick link will take you to the AskNow page at http://www.questionpoint.org/crs/servlet/org.oclc.home. Having accessed the AskNow page, all you will need to do is fill out a brief web form. Details you will need for the web form are:

- your name
- email address—which enables a transcript to be emailed to you after the session with URLs (the email address needs to be confirmed)
- postcode
- information level (this is selected from a dropdown menu)
- the question, then click on Connect.

After you have connected, remain online until a librarian responds to your query. (A survey is sent after the chat session to ensure a quality service.)

Ernie Dingo

In the pursuit of a quote for an Ernie Dingo story for the *cairnseye* magazine in *The Cairns Post*, I found I had exhausted all obvious avenues, which ranged from Cairns music stores selling Slim Dusty CDs and a private vinyl collection of Slim Dusty albums to phoning ABC Far North Qld and checking various library catalogues. Eventually I tried the State Library of Queensland's AskNow real-time reference service. Below is an edited extract of my AskNow chat transcript, to give you an indication of the chat process and the very fast and helpful response.

Chat transcript

Hello, Gail

Chat transcript: Could you please find the correct words to a Slim Dusty song, titled 'Grasshopper: Loose in Queensland'. The words I need checked are: '. . . as big as any goose' and could you supply the complete line that includes these words? Many thanks for any assistance you can provide. Cheers Gail.

Librarian2-NSW: 'Librarian 2-NSW' has joined the session.

Gail: The song title is listed in the ABC Sing Online Index '75–'04.

Librarian2-NSW: Hi Gail, David from the State Library of NSW here. I'll see what I can find.

Librarian2-NSW: *Sing!* was an annual periodical produced by the ABC. Do you know which year this song was in it?

Gail: Librarian 2, yes, the years indicated were 1982 and 1986.

Librarian2-NSW: Yes, we just found it too, it says it's in 1982 and 1986.

Librarian2-NSW: If you don't mind waiting we can pop down to the stacks and have a look for you.

Gail: Great and thanks.

Librarian2-NSW: My colleague has gone to get it, so please wait.

Gail: No problem.

Librarian2-NSW: We have it here, it has the line 'A grasshopper loose, as big as any goose, and he drinks pineapple juice all over Queensland'.

Gail: Librarian 2—Wonderful! Many thanks for all your help.

Librarian2-NSW: Thanks Gail, and thanks for using AskNow.

'LIVING TREASURES'

In every community there are people with astonishing knowledge about issues and events. Finding these 'living treasures' and exploiting their reservoirs of knowledge is an art form. Some reporters have very good contacts because they 'work their sources'. For example, your news editor tells you on Monday morning that you are to write a feature story on the rising tide of youth crime for Saturday's feature section. Make a note of where you would start and whom you would speak to. Sources could include the local police chief, victims support group, school teachers and principals, parents, young people themselves, youth aid workers, community groups and lawyers, politicians and perhaps criminologists or academics interested in youth crime.

During the process of interviewing these sources you will find one or two people significantly more resourceful than others. They will make good copy. They will point you in other directions for information and source material, open doors and provide access for you. Make sure you keep their contact details and telephone or email these 'living treasures' regularly for news tips. These key informants are the lifeblood of journalism. Don't forget these fonts of knowledge may be in your very own newsroom.

RESEARCHERS

Some elite interviewers have the services of a full-time researcher—generally for high-profile television programs. For instance Oprah's 2009 Christmas special interview with President Barack Obama and his wife, Michelle, demonstrated Oprah's researchers had been thorough when she questioned Barack about the community Christmas tree—the decorations of which (more than 800) were sent to various communities throughout the United States, which were asked to decorate them so that they were representative of 'a favorite local landmark' (The White House, The Press Office 2009).

For most journalists, however, the onus is on you to research your own stories.

COMPUTER-ASSISTED REPORTING

Journalists report the news using a plethora of social media or Internet tools such as Facebook, Twitter, Twitpic, Blogs, YouTube and Skype. The Haiti earthquake is a pertinent example as news received worldwide about the devastation was facilitated by Internet-connected tools. This was significant in that Haiti is recognised as the 'poorest nation in the Western Hemisphere' (Paul 2010:1).

It was early Wednesday, 13 January 2010 that this tweet: 'DIGICEL IS WORKING! CALL UR FAMILY NOW!!' was posted by Carel Pedre (a well-known Haitian radio and television presenter) after a 7.0 magnitude earthquake struck Haiti on Tuesday 12 January 2010 (Pedre quoted in Paul 2010:1).

Twitter was one of the primary tools used to disseminate information and photographs about the earthquake in Haiti as well as other disasters on a worldwide basis. 'The *Sydney Morning Herald* reported that images sent via Twitpic and other Twitter-based photo services were hitting the Internet long before news agencies produced anything similar. And as Haitian officials were giving their reports on what happened, eyewitness accounts from Haitians in messages of 140 characters or less were already widespread' (Paul 2010:1).

'I'm hearing singing and praying from the Carrefour Feuilles area. My prayers go out to the folks there' is an example of a tweet by Richard Morse that delivers a very poignant and realistic picture of how the Haitians were dealing with the disaster. Haitifeed, a 'Wordpress-powered blog', is also proving to be a constant source of stories from those who have witnessed the devastation in addition to its use for mainstream media reports. CNN's iReport Desk was also receiving 'reports from citizen journalists', which were screened by the editorial staff. A Facebook group known as Earthquake Haiti also made its presence felt in accumulating in excess of 14,000 members functioning both as a forum for keeping abreast of the latest news and a support group (Paul 2010:1).

Skype was used to communicate with family and relatives worldwide, organisations providing assistance and the media. In a report to the CBS News Pedre candidly says, 'What's not clear, however, is whether Haitians are using these technologies to communicate and help each other. From what I've seen so far, the use of tools like Twitter and Facebook are more helpful for delivering news about Haiti to the outside world instead of aiding those directly affected by the crisis—a recurring theme that we've already seen play out in places like Iran and India' (Pedre in Paul 2010:1-2).

Social media

Internet sites such as Facebook, YouTube and Twitter for reporting and the retrieval of information have had a massive impact on the journalism world. These sites are instantaneous in terms of their application and easily accessed, and are now considered serious journalistic tools that assist in gathering and disseminating news faster than any other form of traditional media.

Additionally, Facebook (http://www.facebook.com) is ideal for promoting yourself on a professional basis, for example if you are a freelance journalist. It can also be useful for contacting others for assistance with difficult stories, and career opportunities, and for consultations with editors. Developing a discussion group pertaining to the area you work in can operate as an active support system and a forum for brainstorming ideas.

Name searches are helpful if you are looking for further biographical material on a prospective interviewee. Searches for co-workers can also be performed either by entering the company's name or the specific name of the person you are seeking.

A 'real-time network', Twitter (http://twitter.com) uses an interface that starts with 140 characters—each character and space deducts from 140 as you type your 'tweet' or message. Therefore in-depth online discussions wouldn't be practical, but as a tool for on-the-spot reporting it works very well. Because of its simplicity Twitter can be used even with the faintest of signals, for instance in rural locations where the signal is weaker, so access using SMS from a mobile phone can be accommodated. A Twitter account also gives you access to Twitpic, enabling photos to be published on the website, your mobile phone or the Twitter network (Twitter 2010:1-3).

While social media tools are immediate in their use, they also work effectively in conjunction with traditional media outlets. For example, televised current affairs programs such as the ABC's *7.30 Report*'s website supplies updated information to Facebook and Twitter subscribers, while Channel Nine's *A Current Affair* website encourages comments via Twitter. Regarding the application of YouTube in tandem with traditional media, this has led to what author Henry Jenkins described as 'convergence culture'.

Convergence culture

Reviewer John Cokley, in examining Henry Jenkins's book *Convergence Culture* (2008), states he focuses on one of the foremost examples 'of collaboration between new and old media institutions—YouTube . . . for grassroots media as well as part of the larger cultural economy' (Cokley 2009: 133). The use of YouTube is advantageous in that its access encompasses local news right through to global news. In his review, Cokley describes YouTube as 'the place where John Citizen meets CNN: it serves as a giant media archive; and it connects a range of other content creation sites' (Cokley 2009: 133–4).

For journalists and writers who embrace the advent of a 'participatory culture' (Cokley 2009: 134) via network computing in order to obtain interviews, access resources and background information, these applications are most certainly enhanced by a 'collective intelligence' (Jenkins 2008: 4 quoted in Cokley 2009: 134).

This 'collective intelligence' is the result of participation across all levels of society, from bloggers, local community groups, welfare organisations and celebrity-fan groups through to educational and national government bodies, and is derived from all those who contribute their skills, expertise and resources using network computing. 'We are learning how to use that power through our day-to-day interactions within convergence culture' and that 'convergence culture represents a shift in the ways we think about our relations to media' (Jenkins 2008: 4, 22 in Cokley 2009: 134).

Cokley's description of YouTube epitomises its identity online as 'a community where people are entertained, informed, educated and inspired through the sharing of video' (YouTube 2010: 2), and furthermore acts as a valuable resource for researchers.

Warning

While computer-assisted research and reporting is fast, immediate and efficient, sole reliance on information from a computer can be enormously risky. As anyone can create and establish a website or upload a video onto YouTube, it is wise to ascertain the credibility of online content used for research.

Journalism sites focusing on new media

The **Poynter Institute** offers many great resources such as tip sheets and bibliographies for journalists all on one site at http://www.poynter.org. An invaluable resource for journalists is the National Institute of Computer-Assisted Reporting (NICAR) at http://data.nicar.org. An allied site is the Investigative Reporters and Editors' (IRE) site at http://www. ire.org. IRE is an organisation that fosters quality investigative journalism on a worldwide basis through the application of training and resources; it is a supportive network for investigative journalists, and promotes journalism excellence. These American websites contain a wealth of ideas and information that is useful to all practitioners.

Need to find a specialist source? One place to start is **ProfNet** at https://profnet.prnewswire.com. It links journalists to academics, professional communicators and other expert sources on the web. To connect quickly to experts on the web, for any subject query there is an easy link to a ProfNet query form. (ProfNet is owned by PR Newswire.)

Finding information fast

The University of Queensland's Belinda Weaver has developed one of the best sources of online information and contacts for journalists in Australia, OZguide. It is located at http://www. journoz.com. It covers everything from government (including Hansard) and non-government organisations to phone directories, all accessed from a 'rounds'-based structure which then links to numerous other sites and home pages.

Please note: other useful sites are included in the Resources section, but remember that websites come and go.

Performing Internet searches

Bruce Grundy, author of *So You Want to be a Journalist?* (2007), recommends the use of Boolean logic to extract useful results when searching the Internet, in preference to finding a vast amount of irrelevant material to sift through. 'The common Boolean terms that computers respond to include AND, OR, NOT, ADJ (adjacent), and WITH' (Grundy 2007: 284). Ways of narrowing your search include capitalisation and using quote marks around terms as a phrase search specific to your query. Note, however, that not all search engines or databases use the same search criteria.

Search engines like Google and Yahoo use Boolean logic to locate information. 'Search engines operate on the basis of defaults which they "insert" between the words you put into their search field. Most now default to AND' (Grundy 2007: 284). Google search queries are identified by the use of square brackets and by including quote marks that create a phrase, for example ['Barack Obama']. The search engine will retrieve only those pages that use the phrase 'Barack Obama'.

Because Google searches according to the sequence of the words that you enter, using the basic search query is not only the easiest search strategy but is also sufficient for a majority of searches.

TIPS

To ascertain useful information on Internet sites:
- Are the Internet sites authoritative or the sources reputable?
- Check whether there is a date available on the website, so that you are aware of when the material was published.
- Is the material on the site current? If it is over two years old it may not be relevant (Grundy 2007: 285).

RESEARCHING FOR INVESTIGATIVE JOURNALISM

> JAKARTA, Indonesia—The closest most people will ever get to remote Papua, or the operations of Freeport-McMoRan, is a computer tour using Google Earth to swoop down over the rainforests and glacier-capped mountains where the American company mines the world's largest gold reserve (Perlez and Bonner 2005: 1).

Reporters are finding innovative uses for the plethora of content available online. Stefan Geens describes the article co-written by *New York Times* journalists Jane Perlez and Raymond Bonner (27 December 2005), entitled 'Below a mountain of wealth, a river of waste', as an 'excellent piece of investigative journalism' but also believes this article represents the arrival of Google Earth journalism (Geens 2005:1).

Google Earth not only succeeds in revealing the extent of mining being undertaken by Freeport (a New Orleans–based company) at the Grasberg mine, but also exposes an improper environmental practice that has resulted in approximately one billion tonnes of mine tailings being allowed to accumulate in a jungle river (Perlez and Bonner 2005: 2).

This use of Google Earth relies upon an assumption that the photographs taken by Google are as authentic and credible as source material as, say, commissioning a pilot to fly over the mine and take aerial photographs. Needless to say, reporters should always take care when using Google Earth or any other online resource, and always seek supporting evidence.

Robert Reid, non-fiction writer and journalist, has authored five non-fiction books and 'has had his work published in several national magazines' (Sedorkin 2009: 19). He has also worked as a media adviser, advertising scriptwriter and for *The Courier-Mail* newspaper as the Cairns Bureau chief as well as teaching creative writing and journalism.

While Robert admits he knows a good story, he's not as enamoured of news writing as he is of feature writing. His 'dogged determination' in pursuing the truth has culminated in a two-part book, *Third Party to Murder: The Sequel,* which resulted in police conducting their seventh investigation into the deaths of two women. Both he and 'the families of those involved [have] never believed the deaths of Atherton [Far North Queensland] women Vicki Arnold and Julie-Anne Leahy in 1991 were the result of a murder-suicide pact' (Sedorkin 2009: 19).

'His five books combine his news ability to dig up the facts with his feature-writing skills of telling a tale in an easy, yet gripping style' (Sedorkin 2009: 19). Of his latest book about sharks, which required reinterviewing experts such as Ben Cropp to update his material, Robert candidly explained, 'I've done a lot of research but I haven't written a word yet ... it's the research that takes the time' (Sedorkin 2009: 18).

REFERENCES

Benitez, G. 24 June 2009, 'WFOR's New iPhone Challenge', pp. 1–2, http://cbs4.com/, accessed 15 February 2010

Cell Phone Digest 27 October 2008, 'Google Earth Now Available for the iPhone and iPod', http://www.cellphone digest.net/, accessed 21 January 2010

Cokley, J. 2009, 'Successor superior to original', *Australian Journalism Review*, vol. 31, no. 1, book review, pp. 133–5, http://www.icahdq.org/aboutica/press/ajr-09a-book reviews.pdf, accessed 8 March 2010

Facebook 2010, 'Facebook: About', http://www.facebook.com/, accessed 15 February 2010

Geens, S. 29 December 2005, 'Google Earth journalism arrives', *Ogle Earth*, pp. 1–3, http://www.ogleearth.com/, accessed 25 January 2010

Grundy, B. 2007, *So You Want to be a Journalist?*, Cambridge University Press, Port Melbourne, Vic

Hill, K. 1996, *Advanced Interviewing Skills for Journalists*, National Diploma in Journalism, Wellington Polytechnic and the Open Polytechnic of New Zealand, quoted with permission from the broadcaster

Investigative Reporters and Editors (IRE), Inc., University of Missouri, Missouri School of Journalism, Columbia, http://www.ire.org/, accessed 3 March 2010

Jenkins, H. 2008, *Convergence Culture: Where old and new media collide*, New York University Press, New York.

National Institute of Computer-Assisted Reporting (NICAR), University of Missouri, Missouri School of Journalism, Columbia, http://data.nicar.org/, accessed 3 March 2010

Paul, I. 14 January 2010, 'Tech tools tell the story of earthquake in Haiti', *PCWorld*, pp. 1–5, http://www.pcworld.idg.com.au/article/332380/, accessed 21 January 2010

Perlez, J. and Bonner, R. 27 December 2005, 'Below a mountain of wealth, a river of waste', NYTimes.com, pp. 1–7, http://www.nytimes.com/, accessed 25 January 2010

Poynter Online, http://www.poynter.org/, accessed 3 March 2010

Profnet, https://profnet.prnewswire.com/, accessed 3 March 2010

Sedorkin, G. 17 September 2008, chat transcript, AskNow, http://www.questionpoint.org/crs/servlet/org.oclc.chat.ClientChatLog, accessed 17 September 2008

——24–30 September 2008, 'Ernie's choice', *The Cairns Post*, *cairnseye*, pp. 10–11

——25–31 March 2009, 'Stranger to fiction', *The Cairns Post*, *cairnseye*, pp. 18–19

State Library of Queensland, AskNow—national chat service,

http://www.questionpoint.org/, accessed 9 January 2010

——http://www.slq.qld.gov.au/, accessed 3 March 2010

The White House, The Press Office 2 December 2009, 'Remarks by The First Lady at Holiday Press Preview', The White House—Office of the First Lady, http://www.whitehouse. gov/, accessed 15 March 2010

Twitter 2010, 'What Twitter Does', http://twitter.com/about, accessed 15 February 2010

Weaver, B. 29 March 2009, Journoz: updates for Australian journalists—last update, The University of Queensland, Brisbane, http://www.journoz.com/, accessed 3 March 2010

YouTube 2010, YouTube—advertise, http://www.youtube.com/ advertise, accessed 15 February 2010

3

GETTING STARTED

> '"But," he said with a wicked smile, "I can fit you in Tuesday at 2 a.m." In that case there was nothing to do but grit my teeth, set my alarm clock, and show up' (Lobsenz 2009: 1).

Norman Lobsenz, a past president of the American Society of Journalists and Authors, in his article about the most common interviewing problems relates his experiences concerning difficult interviewees and interview questions that pose a problem regarding when, what and how to ask. The above quote pertains to a scientist who was interested to see how determined Lobsenz was to obtain the interview. Although the scientist agreed to do the interview, the condition he set might give an interviewer cause to consider whether or not to go ahead. So, as Lobsenz advises, even if the conditions aren't usual, 'Don't argue; just do it' (Lobsenz 2009: 1).

Lobsenz has also found himself surfing in order to obtain an interview. This time it was a case of negotiating with a busy minister who lived in Hawaii when Lobsenz himself had only one day available to conduct this interview. If the subject of the interview is too busy to speak to you at a particular time,

Lobsenz recommends making the effort to find out what they are doing and then arrange to meet them where it is convenient. The result of the 'surfing interview' was that all of Lobsenz's questions were answered!

An interviewer might also encounter the busy traveller. Lobsenz suggests that if you know that the interviewee's trip is a short one, just be on that plane or train. There is nowhere they can hide. Lobsenz's resourcefulness is clearly demonstrated in this particular quote: '(To interview a famous tennis player who was driving to an out-of-town tournament, I managed to hitch a ride in her limo. Taking notes was tricky, but I sorted them out on the train ride home.)' (Lobsenz 2009: 1; original emphasis).

PSYCHING YOURSELF UP FOR THE INTERVIEW

Psyching yourself up for an interview is only one of several techniques and behaviours necessary for getting started as an interviewer. The more preparation you have undertaken for an interview, the more relaxed and efficient you are likely to be. Remember, it is not just new journalists who become nervous before interviews. Even journalists who have conducted hundreds of interviews have their adrenaline pumping as they ask that first question.

Telephone terror or phone phobia is not uncommon and can paralyse reporters who have to ring people they do not know, or when they have to ask 'hard' questions. It is often the inevitability of a creeping deadline and a pushy chief reporter or news editor that forces you to pick up the phone. Deathknock interviews, confrontational interviews in which reporters have to challenge people about what they have said and interviewing witnesses after tragedies all demand courage.

> **TIP**
>
> To help the psyching-up process:
> 1 Take a few deep breaths.
> 2 Rehearse your opening lines to build confidence.
>   Then, just do it!

CONTACTS

One tried and tested aid for getting started as an interviewer is the old faithful—the journalist's contact book. A veteran journalist once offered to sell his contact book to a colleague for $5000. The contact book had such a high value because the journalist religiously sought out and entered the after-hours numbers, mobile phone numbers and holiday address numbers of every single source he ever came into contact with. This scruffy address book, which had to be bound with rubber bands, was locked in the reporter's desk when he was out of the newsroom. A good contact book or electronic list of contacts can mean the difference between getting an interview in time for a deadline and failing to speak to someone who is hot news. Palm Pilots and other electronic files can be useful too, including email contacts.

Start now

Start your list of contacts as soon as you start your first story— whether this is at university, a journalism training course or in the workplace. As soon as you make contact with a source, enter their details in your list. Don't put this task off. You may lose the information and then have to go through the same tedious methods of finding the source the next time you want an interview. Most journalists consider their contact book or list their 'bible' and would be lost without it. It is wise to keep a duplicate copy at home. Make sure your contact list is easy to carry around. To help with future research some journalists include the dates of stories beside the source's names. One way to develop your list of contacts after an interview is to ask your source for any other people who should be contacted for the story. Don't forget to include email addresses for your contacts.

TIP

Use a rating system whereby you put stars against the names of those contacts who supply accurate and timely information to you regularly. The more stars, the better the contact.

TOOLS OF THE TRADE: RECORDING DEVICES AND NOTEPADS

As any reporter who has survived a libel action can testify, journalistic reputation rests on the quality of evidence that can be produced to prove that the interviewee said what was reported. Quality shorthand notes in a notepad and a recording are both good libel insurance. They provide evidence that you didn't misquote the source in an interview or that you didn't 'doctor' quotes. Each form of recording interviews has its advantages and drawbacks. In some newsrooms there is a prescribed protocol for data collection. In others it is up to the individual reporter. In either case the best advice is: be systematic.

Notepads and recordings should be annotated as neatly as possible with the interviewee's name, time and date of interview. After use they should be stored, not lost. If someone disputes an aspect of your story the last thing you want is a frantic hunt through the newsroom, your home or the office car to find your reporter's notepad. It pays to put a unique identifier with a marker pen on the front of your current notepad so that no one else will pick it up by mistake. Print journalist

Jodie Munro O'Brien advises to always have a spare notebook and pen (or two), even on holidays, because 'you just never know when you could find yourself in the middle of breaking news' (personal email interview with Jodie Munro O'Brien).

TIP

Develop a housekeeping system for your interview data. This will provide insurance against trouble, such as claims of misreporting or libel actions. Most newsrooms and news organisations insist that reporters keep interview data for a certain period before it is destroyed.

Recording devices

Recording devices can make some people nervous and self-conscious and inhibit good quotes. But recording an interview does allow the reporter to maintain eye contact with the subject of the interview, and that is valuable for picking up important non-verbal cues. Recording an interview also means that you concentrate on asking the 'right' questions, including succinct follow-up questions, rather than worrying about converting words to shorthand. Disks and flash drives can be time-consuming to transcribe when working to daily print media deadlines but essential to provide voice for radio. Write your story first, then fast-forward through the disk to find the quotes you require. During the interview, take enough notes to make it possible to write the story without the recording, in case it fails and also to give an indication where material will appear.

Whatever you take to record the interview, make sure it works; that your recording device has batteries and is correctly maintained; that the machine is on 'record' when the interview starts; and that the microphone is placed so it can clearly pick up all that is said. Start the device before the interview by recording an 'ident' or identification: the time, the date, the name of the interviewee and your name. Ensuring you have quality audio for radio is essential.

TIP

Don't use the 'voice activated' function of a recording device if it has it, as you tend to lose the first few words as the record function starts up.

Some journalists don't record their interviews because they believe they don't listen as intently, knowing they have the recording to fall back on. They feel this lack of concentrated attention means they might miss clues to future questions or angles. Others believe that recordings provide valuable insurance against accusations of bad reporting. Recording devices can also break down, so ensure that you take sufficient notes or you might return empty-handed. Recorders are banned from parliaments, courts and most tribunals, so it is vital for reporters to learn shorthand.

TIP

When you are taking notes your news radar will tell you when you have been given a good quote or angle. Develop a system whereby you underline or put a star beside the best information as you take it down. This saves a lot of time when searching through your notes later.

Notepads

Shorthand is a cost-effective and relatively fail-safe method of collecting interview data. Many reporters possess idiosyncratic, if not eccentric, shorthand—a blend of shorthand and longhand, abbreviated words and symbols. The average person speaks at approximately 160 words per minute, whereas your shorthand expertise might only be 90 words per minute. Don't try to take down every word; you will not use every word of the whole interview no matter how short the exchange.

BEFORE YOU START

In general an interview should provide the reader, listener or viewer with enough information to answer the proverbial five Ws and one H: Who, What, When, Where, Why and How. The interview should: establish *relevance* (for example, Hollywood movie actor Russell Crowe is home visiting family and promoting his latest movie); be *timely* (conducted either before or during his visit); and capture *interest* (seductive introduction, great 'grab' and sparkling quotes).

Each interview will have its own unique rationale, but some generic lines of inquiry include life and death, motivations, aspirations, past achievements, future challenges, current projects, future prospects, state of humanity, social problems, business and industry concerns, political conflict and personal circumstances. Many great interviews arise from the tension between previous statements and current actions.

TIP

Don't forget that interviews are essentially about what interests us most—people.

Before you get started you need to answer two questions about the interview.

1   What is the point of the interview? You should have the purpose clear in your mind. A lack of focus is one of the main causes of poor interviews. British celebrity interviewer Lynn Barber suggests there is a behavioural

problem about interviewing for some beginner journalists,'simply because they're confused about what they're
doing. They want to be liked; they want to make an impression and find common ground with the interviewee.
Which means they want the interview to be a conversation, a dialogue, the start of a beautiful friendship'
(Barber 1999: xiii). Barber states that journalists must
remember they are there on behalf of the readers.
Highly respected Australian political journalist Laurie
Oakes agrees: 'I don't think an interview can ever be
like a conversation. Conversations are, by definition,
unstructured. If you go to an interview without having
some idea of where it's going and what you want out of
it, it's hopeless. I think you need to plan an interview, to
have a purpose when you start out' (quoted in Wilson
2000: 104).

2   Who should you interview to gather the information? Very
often the right person is obvious; you know the source and
that they have the information. At other times the question
of whom to approach won't be so obvious. In these cases it
is better to start with the management of the organisation,
for example, and be directed to the right person.

In reporting on cultures or religions other than ones you
are familiar with, you may be unclear about whom to approach
for comment. In Australia, it is important to know the tribal
name of Indigenous people and the region of the tribe, and
particularly not to refer to Torres Strait Islanders or Aboriginal
people as one and the same, as they are two distinct peoples.
The protocol on Aboriginal communities requires that journalists approach the tribal Elders first before interviewing other
members of the community. If this system is not followed it
can have major repercussions for the journalist, as well as for
members of the community who spoke to the journalist.

THE NEWS ANGLE

Before you start writing up an interview or going to air you need to decide on the angle for the story. Often the angle hits you instantly, and sometimes there is a wealth of possible introductions. At other times you sit staring at the blank computer screen or repeatedly replay your interview in the hope that inspiration arrives.

TIP

Without looking at your notes, think back to what struck you most—what was most important to you? If you phoned a friend to tell them about the interview, what would you tell them first?

Writing a great news angle is one of the joys and one of the mysteries of journalism. It's easy to identify what isn't a great news angle. These include stories that start with areas which have been examined thoroughly in previous interviews, stories that mumble and stumble their way forward, stories that don't grab readers and stories whose introductions are cluttered with secondary detail, chronology and abstraction.

TIP

To identify a news angle ask yourself:
- What's different or new about the information?
- What details distinguish this story from others of its kind?
- What will 'grab' the attention of readers, listeners or viewers?

In an interview, keep thinking what questions you could ask to support your angle. Lynn Barber (1991) says the best interviews should sing the strangeness and variety of the human race. What questions will elicit this strangeness and variety? Because journalism is a competitive business you will often be operating against reporters from rival organisations. What will make your interview with a visiting celebrity, for example, different from the rest of the media? Your aim is to walk away with extra information the other journalists didn't get. A tip here is to hold back an original question and ask it after the formal media conference has ended when other journalists can't use the answer.

Remember, sometimes the news editor or chief reporter wants a particular 'angle' out of an interview because your report will be part of a story, or reaction to other comment. They need the information as quickly as possible, and it is your first responsibility to get back to the newsroom with the information speedily. But never close your mind to an unexpected different snippet of information that reveals a new facet to the story.

However, there can be exceptions when it comes to decisions about the news angle. The decision in this case made by CBS executives not to interview Tiger Woods, Sunday 21 March 2010 (and not on record) was 'less as a journalistic stand against an interview subject trying to control questioning than as a practical decision about what benefit the network could get from the interview ... given the restrictions on the interview—five minutes total with Mr Woods, who was declaring several areas of questioning too personal to answer directly—CBS was not likely to be able to get much more information from Mr Woods than either of the sports cable channels', ESPN and the Golf Channel (Carter 2010: 2).

WRITING QUESTIONS AND KEYWORDS

Journalists are almost equally divided over whether having a prepared list of questions is a good idea or not. Some always prepare a list of written questions, but it is only to use as a prop. Other journalists believe that with a formal list of questions you risk limiting your news antennae to the assumptions expressed in the written questions. There is also a risk that you will not follow up on newsworthy answers with further prompts because you are slavishly tied to the questions on the prepared list. They argue that with a list you risk destroying the flow of an interview because the interviewer will not move away from the prepared, but predictable, questions towards what might be special and different that is signalled in the interviewee's previous answers. Others, particularly reporters who conduct profile, personality or extended interviews, suggest that it is unprofessional not to have prepared questions, even if they are not all used during the interview. Journalists with less experience are advised to develop lists of questions. They help boost confidence, the process of devising them encourages good research habits, and prepared questions do focus the interview.

There are two parts to preparing a question line:

1   work out the general topic areas you want to cover, and
2   prepare specific questions.

Keywords or catch phrases can be developed to remind you of general topic areas. For example, before an interview with visiting British journalist John Pilger, the following series of keywords and phrases would help keep general topic areas in mind:

* role of journalist–activist v. reflector
* state of news generally
* international response to investigative journalism
* personal safety in dangerous locations
* controversy over the Pilger style

- current projects
- future projects
- past, present and future—East Timor, Vietnam, race relations in Australia and Iraq.

Whether you have a set of keywords or a prepared list of questions you need to be thinking ahead as the interview unfolds.

ORGANISING YOURSELF

Organising yourself before the interview is another important aspect of getting started. Here are four organisational tips.

1　Dress appropriately for the interview context. If you are interviewing political or business leaders a suit and tie or sports jacket for men and business clothes for women should be worn. Smart dress is also expected of court reporters. Other contexts may require different dress styles. For example, female reporters covering a Maori tangi funeral should dress in black and wear a long skirt if possible to acknowledge Maori custom at a funeral. A female reporter once gained an exclusive interview during the Mr Asia drug case with notorious New Zealand criminal Peter Fulcher at his heavily secured North Shore house. She had to go alone and wore jeans and running shoes for convenience and a quick escape if necessary. However, you would be expected to wear something smarter if you were interviewing celebrities at the Golden Globe or Aria awards.

2　Have maps, addresses, telephone contacts and all the destination details with you when setting out on an interview assignment. Don't rely on photographers or other members of the camera crew to know where you should be going. Being late for an interview will definitely start things off on the wrong foot. If there is no time, use Google Earth or Global Positioning System (GPS).

3   Let the newsroom know where you are at all times, and alert them to whether or not you have the story as the deadline looms or if the angle of the story has changed. Your information or quotes from an interview may be vital for the front-page lead or the hourly bulletin and can be read back over a mobile or satellite phone.

4   Be aware that you might have to go out quickly to interview disaster victims, witnesses to an emergency, or to a spot news event. Develop an 'on call' persona so that the chief reporter or news editor chooses you for the unexpected and interesting interview assignments. This state of suspended adrenaline is half the fun of being a reporter.

TIP

As a general rule, don't supply questions in advance to people you are about to interview. If you do, you risk losing the element of surprise essential in many media interviews, and it can allow interviewees to manage and 'spin' their responses. It can also inhibit spontaneity when you are seeking colourful quotes.

ACCESSING THE INTERVIEW

Gaining access to the person you want to interview can be as simple as calling a telephone number. It can also be a major challenge.

Making appointments

For many routine stories reporters can make a timely appointment on the day with a local official, business person or police chief for an interview to gather information for a story.

Punctuality, courtesy and keeping faith by turning up, and conducting an interview efficiently to minimise time inconvenience to the interviewee become second nature to reporters writing routine news stories. But what happens when you can't get past a gatekeeper, an overly protective secretary or an officious minder?

Dropping in unannounced

Using surprise tactics is a familiar journalistic technique for getting to people who don't want to talk to you. Going to someone's office and asking for comment, waiting in a carpark beside a car or staking out an airport entrance or the side door of a courtroom are regular practices for reporters, photographers and camera crews. There is no universally successful formula for getting someone who doesn't want to speak or comment, even though gathering all sides of a story is enshrined as a fundamental principle of journalistic fairness. There is a measure of luck involved in gaining access to a reluctant interviewee. But it is far more likely that persistence rather than luck wins the story.

TIPS

To get past the gatekeepers:
- Be persistent and don't give up.
- If the gatekeeper won't put you through on the telephone after the first and second attempts, then try to get a letter, facsimile or email to the person who is being protected. In some cases the potential source of the news really doesn't mind talking to reporters, and the gatekeeper simply assumes the role of keeping you out.
- In exceptional cases it may be appropriate to drop off a list of written questions that would form the basis of the interview. Then, if the source still will

---

not comment, the questions can be referred to in the story with the phrase that 'such and such was unavailable for comment'.

- If it is appropriate (check with your chief-of-staff) the gatekeeper should be told politely but firmly that it is in the public interest that the information be sought and that stonewalling is unacceptable.

- Always try to find the mobile phone numbers of potential sources of news. These are numbers they usually answer themselves. You may find yourself getting straight through to the prime minister, the bikie gang leader, the shy sports star or the elusive celebrity.

- Remember that ministerial press secretaries paid by the public purse are expected to provide access and act as a link between Cabinet ministers and the media. You are entitled to remind them of their obligations if they are overly protective and try to shut you out.

THE GOOD, THE BAD AND THE UGLY: DEALING WITH PUBLIC RELATIONS PRACTITIONERS

The higher the stakes in politics, professional sport and corporate business the more likely there is to be a professional media minder 'guarding' the sources of news. Journalists need to learn how to deal with PR people and combat their strategies if they are to get stories.

The good

In instances such as civil defence emergencies where the public relations spokesperson is the conduit for information, or where police media relations officers are handling spot crime news, a strong relationship of trust and reciprocity can develop between

journalists and PR people. The majority of public relations practitioners see their job altruistically as a positive influence between
clients as sources of the news and the news media. In some cases
such as the police, fire service or other emergency services the
public relations spokesperson is trained in the service they
represent and simply want to present it in the best possible light.

TIP

Use PR people to:
- provide background information
- arrange access for the interview
- indicate where sources can be found for comment
- provide one perspective on the news.

The bad

Most organisations and CEOs are now trained in working with
the media and in crisis communications. Those in the PR profes-
sion understand that it is better to get correct information out
quickly than to fuel speculation.

Tension will always exist between journalists and PR
people simply because PR is a barrier between reporters and
direct sources of the news. Who wants to interview a celebrity's minder or a politician's 'spin doctor' who is putting a
biased angle on the politician's message? The public expects the
real thing. Despite the rapid growth of the news management
business, the public, too, retains a healthy scepticism about PR.

TIP

Do not allow PR people to:
- dictate the terms and conditions of an interview
- spin the angles in your news story
- provide the question
- deny you legitimate access to an interviewee.

And the ugly

Two American researchers, James Tankard and Randy Sumpter (1993), make the worrying claim that journalists are becoming more and more accepting of spin doctors. They maintain that this is disturbing when you think about what spin doctors do, which is to try to manipulate the slant, angle or frame that will be used in news reports. That should be the job of the journalist and not a source with a vested interest. It is clear, too, that in a number of areas, particularly politics, sport, big business and former government agencies that have been corporatised, such as health boards in New Zealand and Telstra in Australia, there is a growing imbalance in resources between newsrooms and the PR machine.

Good journalists constantly fight to maintain the independence and autonomy of their news. So always ask yourself:

- What's the spin here?
- Have I too freely accepted the PR version?
- Have I spoken to a range of other sources?
- Will an interview with someone else provide a truer picture?

TIPS

1   Always try for your own interview with a source named in a supplied press release. This is superior to a simple rewrite of someone else's work, and allows you to double-check the contents. It also means you are not hostage to the 'spin'.

2   Consult other reporters and the codes of ethics that apply to you before accepting benefits, favours and perks from PR people. Gifts, liquor, travel and tickets to shows and sporting events might not appear to be a problem until a favour is expected of you in return.

REFERENCES

Barber, L. 1991, *Mostly Men*, Viking, London, UK

—— 1999, *The Demon Barber*, Penguin, London, UK

Carter, B. 22 March 2010, 'Why CBS said no to Tiger Woods interview', *NYTimes.com*, Media Decoder Blog, pp. 1-7, http://mediadecoder.blogs.nytimes.com/, accessed 23 March 2010

Lobsenz, N. 1 May 2009, 'The most common interview problems: and how to get around them', *The Writer*, vol. 122, no. 5, pp. 32-3, http://www.writermag.com; Australian/New Zealand Reference Centre database, Accession no. 37365139, pp.1-2, accessed 21 January 2010

Tankard, J.W. and Sumpter, R. 1993, 'Media awareness of media manipulation: the use of the term "spin doctor"', paper presented to the Mass Communication and Society Division of the Association for Education in Journalism and Mass Communication, Kansas City, MO

Wilson, R. 2000, *A Big Ask: Interviews with Interviewers*, New Holland Publishers, Sydney, NSW

4 BREAKING THE ICE

Anyone who conducts interviews regularly will undoubtedly tell you that the first few minutes of the interview are the most crucial. This is the 'first impressions' time that can make or break an interview. It's this informal time before an interview that sets the atmosphere and the tone, and is the time to establish a rapport with the interviewee. These first few minutes are critical and can be the key to a great interview—or, in some cases, getting an interview at all. A common technique to get the conversation rolling is known as an icebreaker. It can take anywhere from ten seconds to ten minutes, sometimes longer, but is an essential start to any interview.

Icebreakers can be divided into two main categories:

1 research icebreakers, and
2 on-the-spot icebreakers.

Research icebreakers are devised as a result of the journalist's knowledge of, and research on, the interviewee. These icebreakers are preferable and are one preparation technique that is practically guaranteed to produce positive results. If it is a spontaneous event, which does not allow the luxury of time for research, the interviewer must then rely on their observation skills or general knowledge to formulate an on-the-spot icebreaker.

Australian journalist Peter Davis recalls using a joke as an icebreaker when he was interviewing a reluctant Queen's Counsel.

He would only do the interview at his chambers, which immediately put me at a disadvantage. In the studio I'm comfortable—but I definitely wasn't in his imposing chambers. As soon as I sat down he said: 'I won't talk about my law firm and I won't talk about my family'. So my first question was: 'How much money does your firm bring in each week and how many illegitimate children do you have?' It certainly broke the ice! (personal interview with Peter Davis).

BEFORE THE ICEBREAKER

Before you get to use your icebreaker, your initial contact with the interviewee should be polite but confident. Shake hands firmly (without crushing bones), introduce yourself and greet your interviewee. Australian political journalist Kerry O'Brien believes it's a straightforward courtesy to shake a person's hand when you meet them for the first time, or if you're welcoming somebody into your studio or into your domain. 'I think it's only sensible unless you're dealing with an axe murderer who's just been recaptured.'

There's an onus on you to offer basic courtesies of politeness. I think it's in your interest for a better outcome if you can make that person feel comfortable. But you don't have to be obsequious, in fact I would hope that you wouldn't be. And you don't have to be too deferential. A straight-forward handshake is enough, then if it's the Prime Minister, you might say 'thank you for coming in to the studio Prime Minister'. I think you can apply that equally to most people in most situations unless they've signalled to you that they wanted you to call them by their first name. If it's somebody who is so familiar—like Tiger Woods—you'd feel a little bit silly saying Mr Woods when the world calls him Tiger. Use your instincts in that regard (personal interview with Kerry O'Brien).

WHEN?

The time for your icebreaker is before the actual formal inter-view but after the initial introduction has been made. It should give you a chance to gauge how the interviewee is feeling about the exchange and to put everyone at ease (including yourself). This is not the time to bring out your recording devices, camera or notepad, particularly if the interviewee appears uncertain about the exchange. This is also not the time to start asking questions or discussing areas that are critical to your interview. If your interviewee is still looking uncomfortable or threatened after your initial icebreaker, don't launch into your interview regardless. Keep the conversation going; even if this takes ten minutes or more, it will pay off in the end.

WHO?

If the interviewee is someone you call on frequently as a source or is experienced in dealing with the news media, less time needs to be devoted to the icebreaker. Establishing a rapport is always important, but busy people in public life value their time and expect an interview to be conducted quickly and efficiently. Unnecessary chit-chat will be seen as time-wasting and not conducive to an effective interview. Electronic journalists seeking a short news grab would rarely spend time on icebreakers, unless the person was inexperienced with the media.

Young people can be particularly difficult to interview. Often they are self-conscious and prone to one-word answers. Taking time to establish a rapport by asking 'easy' questions about their age, school and interests can give them the confidence to be more expansive in their interview answers. One feature writer recalled an interview with a shy 14-year-old athlete who was clearly nervous and reluctant to talk. 'I began with a series of questions about his age, what form he was in, how long he had been competing, the name of his coach. He found them easy to answer and loosened up a lot. The interview went well after that.'

CULTURAL CONCERNS

Members of Pacific Island communities who have been under-reported in the mainstream media will often be apprehensive, if not suspicious, of journalists. Explaining the purpose of the story and why the interview is essential can allay justified concerns and facilitate a successful interview.

Members of Aboriginal communities might be concerned that the journalist intends concentrating only on negative stereotypes, so some time should be spent with the tribal Elders explaining the aim of the interview and how it will be used in the final story.

If you are interviewing someone from another culture it is essential, if you don't already have the background knowledge, to research conversational 'dos' and 'don'ts'. For instance, if you were interviewing someone from the Torres Strait Islands, you should find out exactly which island they are from, as each has its own diverse history and culture. If they are from Moa Island, for instance, get a map and find out exactly where it is, and research basic information about the island and its people before the interview. With Maori, it is important to establish their 'iwi' (tribe) and then show that you know where it is based. With Pacific Island and Asian communities it is essential to recognise and appreciate national identity and difference. Journalists who don't may cause offence.

RESEARCH ICEBREAKERS

Bruce Grundy, author of *So You Want to be a Journalist* (2007), indicates that it is advisable, if you can't find any background information on a prospective interviewee, to admit it. However, if the interviewee does have a sports background, for example, then 'be professional' and perform your research (Grundy 2007: 320). The Internet can be the best place to start, particularly if looking for biographies.

Those who interview regularly agree that *homework* always pays off when it comes to icebreakers, and in fact interviews as a whole. As Melbourne's *Herald Sun* associate editor John Hamilton points out: 'Say you're about to interview a public figure and you do your reading and you do your homework and you find, for example, in a small cutting somewhere that the person reads science fiction. If you just pop this into the conversation and say: "I understand you've got an interest in science fiction?" they go, "Crikey, you know a bit about me". It flatters them, and people respond to flattery' (personal interview with John Hamilton).

Understandably the interviewee would be impressed that you have gone to the trouble to find out about them and their interests. A similar instance many years ago involved a radio journalist who had to interview a conservationist and television personality about a talk he was giving on sustainable development (not a common topic at the time). The journalist read widely, including getting a copy of the talk from the last venue where the interviewee had spoken. The subject had planned to talk for about fifteen minutes but, when he realised the journalist had gone to some trouble (and actually said as much to the journalist), the interview continued for almost two hours.

If you know someone is interested in surfing, skiing, photography or any other sport or recreation, this can be very useful, particularly if you share the interest and can talk knowledgeably about it. If you keep up to date with current affairs (which should always be the case with journalists), you could comment on a recent issue or event to break the ice. Be wary about making political comments, though, as this could have the reverse effect and make the atmosphere very frosty. It may also set you up for accusations of bias.

You and the interviewee may have a mutual friend, acquaintance or colleague, and a greeting from them will certainly get things started on a good note. Again, a word of caution: ensure that they are definitely on friendly terms before you start namedropping. Another way to shut down an interview is to express doubt or disapproval. Making a judgemental response will probably cause offence. Equally, you should not be disingenuous and make false expressions of approval. The best approach is to be as objective as possible.

ON-THE-SPOT ICEBREAKERS

Unfortunately you do not always have the time to research the subject of an interview, particularly if it is the result of a spontaneous event or an unexpected opportunity. This is when you must call on your general knowledge or powers of observation to formulate on-the-spot icebreakers. If all else fails comment on the weather, but this is definitely a last resort.

Master of the icebreaker Andrew Urban (right) *with cameraman Greg Kay, recording interviews for* Front Up.
(Photo by Louise Keller, courtesy of SBS Publicity)

Regularly described as one of Australian television's best interviewers, Andrew Urban is a master of the icebreaker. In the SBS television series *Front Up* he literally 'fronts up' to people on the street, in cafés and other assorted locations and starts talking to them. In a very short time Andrew is able to put the interviewees so at ease that they reveal a variety of aspects about their public and private lives.

Because he has never met the interviewees before—in fact he does not even know their names until he approaches them—Andrew relies totally on his powers of observation. For instance, if he sees someone polishing the brass on their boat at the marina, the icebreaker will be based on the boat and may eventually include a request to come aboard and take a closer look. The same goes for motorcycles, bicycles, books, tattoos, bags of shopping and a continually changing assortment of conversation starters.

Andrew says you need to establish a rapport before the interview can begin—and the key is to start with something that the subject is comfortable with.

It's not important what it is—just a very general question. For instance: 'Why are you wearing a purple top?' And you might reply: 'Because it's my mother's favourite colour.' And that would lead me into asking about your mother, and get the conversation started in a non-threatening way (personal interview with Andrew Urban).

The Herald Sun's *John Hamilton with Dame Elisabeth Murdoch, using the surroundings of her property, Cruden Farm, for an on-the-spot icebreaker.* (Photo by Craig Borrow, courtesy of the *Herald Sun*)

Once you're inside a subject's home there are good opportunities for further icebreakers, as the surroundings tend to reflect the sort of person they are. Items such as ornaments, paintings, photographs and sporting trophies are obvious conversation starters. Pets are a particularly easy way to get acquainted, especially if you share their passion for cats, dogs, birds or snakes. A great clue to a person is books.

Books on the shelf or books they are currently reading. Not only are these books good conversation starters, but they help to build a picture of the person you are talking to, which is particularly helpful for feature pieces (personal interview with John Hamilton).

If you're in an office you might comment on the view (if there is one), but if the location is neutral perhaps you might comment on their jewellery, their watch or some other personal effect. Avoid concentrating too much on their personal appearance, though. Andrew Urban will often use appearance as an icebreaker, but stresses that you must approach the topic in a positive way.

For instance you don't say: 'Where did you get that ridiculous haircut from?' and still expect the person to be willing to continue. However, I would say something like: 'That's an interesting haircut. Can you tell me a little bit about that?', in a positive tone, making it obvious I was curious but not critical (personal interview with Andrew Urban).

Studio locations can be daunting, and a good way to break the ice is to empathise with the talent's nervousness. Make a joke about how hot the lights get in a television studio, or how all the equipment in the radio studio scares most journalists. This is the one time when the interviewer can talk about their experiences and background, using it as a way to put the interviewee at ease.

One radio journalist started a difficult interview by confessing her (genuine) fear of all the studio equipment and some of her early mistakes. It not only showed a more personal side to the journalist, but also broke the ice with a few laughs. No matter what technique you use for your icebreaker, there is no substitute for genuine interest and enthusiasm. There are not too many people who do not enjoy telling their story, particularly to a good listener. Make sure it is obvious right from the start that you want to hear their story.

TIPS

- Do your homework.
- Choose something from your research, but not an area critical to the actual interview.
- Good on-the-spot icebreakers can involve remarks about books, the garden, trophies, paintings, pets or photographs.
- Keep up to date with current affairs as a way of breaking the ice.
- Know cultural 'dos' and 'don'ts'.
- Don't be too personal; an interesting watch or piece of jewellery should be reasonably safe.
- The last resort—comment on the weather!

REFERENCES

Grundy, B. 2007, *So You Want to be a Journalist?*, Cambridge University Press, Port Melbourne, Vic

5 THE QUESTIONS

First-time interviewer Beth Harvey of The Cairns Post *believes in being prepared.*

First-time interviewer Beth Harvey admitted to 'blinding excitement' when she found out she was to interview Chaske Spencer (Sam Uley) and Tinsel Korey (Emily Young) of *New Moon* (the second of the *Twilight Saga* vampire films) fame: 'I loved the book so much I called up everyone. But I didn't expect to do someone high profile for my first interview' (personal interview with Beth Harvey). Beth admits it was a bit 'overwhelming and intimidating', but she researched and planned every aspect to 'control my nerves. I was so organised that even if I blanked I could just go to my questions.' Beth was also determined to ask some questions that would be new to the stars. During her extensive research she discovered that Tinsel had got in touch and spent time with people from the Quileute and Makah nations depicted in the *Twilight Saga*—so this in turn became one of Beth's questions.

'Q6: Not many people realise that the Quileute Nation is a real community with real people. What did you do to get in touch with the Quileute community? How do they respond to the phenomenon?' Beth said she also ensured with her research that she knew the answers to every question that she asked (personal interview with Beth Harvey).

A cadet journalist recalling one of her very first interviews with an overwhelming businessman said she hadn't prepared very well and was too afraid to ask any questions. After waiting a few minutes while she fumbled around trying to get started, the businessman asked, 'Do you take shorthand?' to which the journalist replied, 'Yes.'

'Well, take this down then,' he said, and then proceeded to dictate a story to the journalist, including quotes and full punctuation—right down to the very last full stop. It was a hard lesson, but the journalist said she always comes completely prepared now, and she always asks questions no matter how daunting the interviewee.

Remain professional at *all* times, no matter what. Follow the basics but always finish off any and every single interview—whether it's an in-depth feature or a quick, short pic story—with: 'Is there anything else you would like to add?' Sometimes this last question ends up with information that turns into the lead paragraph or the focus of the entire story! (personal email interview with Jodie Munro O'Brien).

Though it can be difficult sometimes, you must always ask questions, otherwise you could be treated as a secretary taking down a prepared speech. Your preparation time should include your background research, as well as thinking through your questions and writing them down. Australian political journalist Kerry O'Brien believes that you should always write down your questions because:

Questions help you to focus your attention on the essence of the story or interview. They also help you to order your thoughts in a logical flow, and in framing the question you are also endeavouring to think through what kind of answer the person will give. And that then becomes part of the flow into the next question (personal interview with Kerry O'Brien).

However, Kerry warns:

Many interviewers before me have talked about the trap of sticking to your questions regardless of the answers. And even though you've got your questions prepared, and even though a part of you (whether you like it or not) will be thinking about what you're going to ask next, you've also got to be listening to the answers, and you've got to be processing the answers as you go. You've got to be prepared to throw your questions to one side, or even move from Question 2 to Question 6, because of something that the interviewee has said that demands logically that you go to Question 6. Then you might have to retrace back to Question 4 rather than Question 3, or you might be jettisoning Question 3 altogether (personal interview with Kerry O'Brien).

Kerry O'Brien believes the 'old fundamentals' (the five Ws and one H) will almost always get you through. 'If you come back from any assignment and haven't answered those—to some degree at least—then I hope it's because people have refused to give it to you, not because you have failed to ask' (personal interview with Kerry O'Brien). He also feels it's important to understand the difference between what people want to say and what you, on behalf of your audience, should be getting from them.

> I think it's valid enough for many people to be seeking to use various media outlets as a forum for their ideas, but equally they should expect and understand that it's your job as a journalist to be there on behalf of the audience, not to help them. So if they've got interesting, important things to say without too much prodding on your part—fine. If you can vouch for the veracity of it, the essential truth of it, fine. But in many instances you've got to be there as the check and balance of what's being said. You're not a cipher, you're not somebody's platform, you're not just there for someone to stand on and cast their message out unchecked. I think the bulk of people will want you to show some respect, they'll want you to show common courtesies, but they also want you to be their representative asking the tough questions and keeping people honest.
>
> You're there as the vehicle for the flow of information— but not an unquestioning vehicle (personal interview with Kerry O'Brien).

Whether you are reporting for a news brief or a cover story, you should always be interested in your interviewee—and show it. This should be clear in both your verbal and non-verbal techniques. The simple technique of asking informed questions, then listening to the answers for cues for the next question, is the best way to display interest. Questioning techniques can be divided into three main areas:

1   questions to use
2   questions to try
3   questions to avoid.

CASE STUDY: To explore these various techniques we will use the example of an interview with a bank official conducting a tour of small country branches.

DO ASK the 'who cares' question

One of the essential news values is *consequence*—in other words, a story must be significant or affect people to be newsworthy. Generally the more people who are affected by a story, the larger the story and the closer it will appear to the top of the bulletin or to page 1 of the newspaper. News editors will apply the 'who cares' principle when deciding where your story will be placed and how long it will be, so you should have the answer when you return from the interview. With the bank story it would be essential to determine not only how many branches would be involved in the tour, but also the extent of the region (including population) that would be affected if any changes were made as a result of the visit.

Examples

Q: You're visiting 30 branches. How many people are employed in total?
Q: What are the major regions serviced?
Q: How many customers are involved?

DO USE closed questions but not too often

These are the questions that require only a very limited response—usually a 'yes' or 'no'.

Examples

Q: Have you conducted a tour like this before?
Q: Have you been to these areas before?

If your subject is not particularly forthcoming and is inclined towards giving short answers, using closed questions will not help. Generally journalists are discouraged from using closed questions, but they can come in handy if you want a definitive answer. During the interview with the bank official visiting the branches, it would be useful to ask: 'Are you going to close any branches as a result of your tour?' If the answer is 'no', it should be kept on record in case there is a change of heart in the future. If the answer is 'yes', you have a front-page story.

DO USE open questions for more information

Closed questions are easily converted into open questions—the sort of questions that require more than a yes or no answer. By the simple addition of one of the six essential questions (Five Ws and one H), the question is opened up and should ensure longer answers.

Example

The closed question:

Q: Do you hope to visit a number of branches during your tour?

(which would probably only elicit a yes or no answer) is easily converted into six open questions that ask for longer and more interesting responses.

Q: *Who* will you meet during the tour?
Q: *What* do you hope to achieve?
Q: *When* will you be touring?
Q: *Where* will your tour take you?
Q: *How* will this benefit the public?
Q: *Why* have you chosen this region?

The 'how' and the 'why' questions will generally elicit the most in-depth information and are usually saved for more investigative pieces or longer current affairs stories.

DO USE short precise questions that are easy to answer

American journalist and author of *Interviews that Work* (1986) Shirley Biagi says questions that are longer than three lines are too long. Unless some background explanation is required, three lines is a maximum—particularly for broadcast interviews. In fact, the shorter the better. A sage piece of advice given to a print journalist moving into radio was that the audience has tuned in to hear the person being interviewed—not the journalist. This is also the case with print interviews—the interviewee should not have to interrupt the interviewer to make a response. Some broadcast journalists have been known to ask questions of more than forty-five seconds—sometimes up to one minute. This is far too long.

Example

Instead of asking:

Q: This bank tour is said to be far more extensive than others that have been conducted in the past, which have not resulted in any significant changes and have just been fact-finding missions with no outcomes. What results do you expect from this tour?

why not ask:

Q: What results do you expect this time?

DO USE the 'bigger, brighter, better' question

A lot of interviews should present 'must ask' questions for the journalist. These are the sort of questions the public would want to ask if they were conducting the interview themselves. For instance, an interview with a police detective about a drug raid invites the 'bigger, brighter, better' question. The curious journalist should be wondering: what makes this raid different, special, unusual or worthy of coverage? What gives it that newsworthy angle? If these questions are forgotten a good angle is lost.

Example

Q: Is this the biggest drug raid in this area/state/country?

A 'Yes' answer to this question could easily result in a front-page story.

DO USE the challenge or investigative question

Many answers, particularly those given by people used to dealing with the media, should not go unchallenged. However, if you do want to investigate an answer it is advisable to do your research first.

Example

For instance, let's say the bank official answered your closed question—Are you going to close any branches as a result of your tour?—with a definite 'no'. However, your research found that a similar tour five years earlier resulted in the closure of four branches and the loss of fifteen jobs. Knowing this you *must* ask:

Q: When you toured five years ago you also promised no closures or job losses. Four branches were closed and fifteen people retrenched. What makes this time different?

The official will either explain the difference, if there is one, or ask for the evidence that backs up your 'statement question'. You must be able to provide this. Without proof, a statement like this could get you into a lot of trouble or leave you looking foolish.

DO USE a summary for more information

This technique requires the interviewee to agree or disagree with information you have summarised. As a device to clarify and sometimes to extract a definitive answer, the summary can be a very efficient tool. Instead of getting a 'yes' or 'no' to just one closed question, the summary contains much more information with which the interviewee either agrees or disagrees. Australian journalist Jana Wendt used this technique very effectively in an interview with media owner Rupert Murdoch on the first edition of Channel 7's former current affairs program *Witness*. She used summarisation to clarify the current position of business dealings being conducted between Murdoch and rival media tycoon Kerry Packer.

At the height of the Super League battle (caused by Rupert Murdoch's proposal of a 'super' league that split the existing league, then merged with the ARL to form the NRL) Packer had agreed to help make the peace within rugby league in Australia in return for some broadcast rights and access to Murdoch's Fox movies for his Nine Network.

> JW: Let me talk then about this arrangement, this deal that you had with Mr Packer, or thought you had. Did you shake hands on this deal?
> RM: Of course.
> …
> JW: But if I can just summarise your view of it, since Mr Packer did not deliver on his side of the bargain, presumably you don't want to deliver on your side?
> RM: I think that would be a fair summarisation, yes (Channel 7 1996).

DO USE questions that ask for summaries, rankings or choices

An excellent way to obtain more definitive answers is to ask the interviewee to provide their own summary, to rank information they have been given, or to make a choice. Not only does this provide more detail but it also gives their order of priority or importance.

Examples

For instance, the bank official could be asked for a summary:

Q: Could you summarise the main reasons for this tour?

then to rank the summary:

Q: Could you put those four reasons in order of importance for your company?

and then to make a choice:

Q: What do you believe is the most important reason for looking at these country branches?

DO USE requests for clarification by repeating the answer

The best interviews are the ones in which journalists are listening intently, then using the interviewee's answers to lead into the next question. Taking this point even further, the actual words of the answer can be used to formulate the next question. This is a useful technique for ensuring that you have heard correctly, and for stressing the importance of the answer.

Example

In the interview with the bank official visiting the country branches try:

Q: What changes do you expect to result from your report?
A: I expect there could be changes in staffing levels and the services provided.
Q: Staffing levels could be changed. How?

DO USE

- The 'who cares' question
- Closed questions (but not too often)
- Open questions for more information
- Short precise questions that are easy to answer
- The 'bigger, brighter, better' question
- The challenge or investigative question
- A summary for more information
- Questions that ask for summaries, rankings or choices
- Requests for clarification by repeating the answer

DO TRY repeating or rephrasing questions

Repeating or rewording questions might work with the interviewee who doesn't deal with the media very often, but politicians and business leaders pick up on this technique very quickly. They are just as likely to point out that it doesn't matter how many times you repeat the question or rephrase it, they are not going to answer.

Examples

Q: You said staffing levels could change as a result of the study. How?

A: I really can't answer that until it has been conducted.

Q: Are you trying to say that staff may be put off?

A: No, I'm not saying that at all. I can't say what will happen until we look at the branches.

Q: Do you have any indication that the branches in this region are overstaffed?

A: Again, no, not until we do the research.

Kerry O'Brien believes that, if you're confident of your topic, which generally comes from preparation, repeating questions is a valid technique.

> Whether it's the prime minister, the opposition leader or the treasurer, they are, in the end, also only people. They have their own insecurities, and their own doubts, as well as their own confidence. Yes, they come armed with media skills that have been well honed over years, and yes, they have the capacity to sidetrack, and to spin-doctor, and all of these other things.
>
> But if you have listened carefully to the answers, and it is clear to you that they have not answered your questions, then even though you feel that you're a junior journalist and they're a heavyweight, you can, in a reasonable tone, point out that they haven't answered the question. You can say 'Could I just remind you of what the question was?' without being aggressive (personal interview with Kerry O'Brien).

If your interviewee does not understand your question, they might ask you to reword it or to clarify what you want. This could mean your questions are too wordy. Remember: the interview is not a contest, it is a means of obtaining information from a source for publication. Don't make it too difficult, either for the interviewee or your audience, by using complex words, jargon or overly long statements or questions.

DO TRY posing a hypothetical question

Most interviewees would have difficulty answering the hypothetical question, and many will refuse to tackle a problem that might never arise. Those who have attended 'managing the media' sessions are trained to refuse to answer these questions.

Example

For instance, with our bank official, you might try:

Q: What will you do if bank staff around the country go on strike as a result of your recommendations?

but the official is likely to answer:

A: I think this is a highly unlikely scenario, which I'd prefer not to discuss.

DO TRY playing the devil's advocate

While you may agree with the interviewee, it is a useful technique to challenge them and their answers. This provides the opportunity for a more balanced coverage of the issue. Quite often you can state quite clearly what you are doing.

Example

Q: If I could just play the devil's advocate here . . . Don't you think the criteria you are using to judge the viability of the branches is unfair?

Kerry O'Brien believes playing devil's advocate is a good approach to an interview.

> You don't have to be aggressive about it. If it's a politician or an advocate for any cause, I think it's important for an audience to feel that these people's claims have been tested. That's part of what you're there for. And obviously you can't really test a person unless you've got some understanding of what they're talking about—which goes back to your research and preparation (personal interview with Kerry O'Brien).

DO TRY the tough question

Asking the tough question—or dropping the bomb—is not for the first-time interviewer or the faint-hearted. It is difficult asking the hard question, but most journalists feel it is only fair to give the interviewee the opportunity to give their side of the story or to answer criticism.

The late Paul Lyneham, an award-winning television journalist, believed it could be very difficult asking the hard question, but essential when you feel an injustice has been done or that the interviewee has a case to answer. In the following anecdote, he recalled one instance of how he coped with asking the difficult question.

Paul Lyneham, courtesy of the Nine Network.

My most famous recollection of that dilemma was a story I was doing for *Four Corners* and we spent three days filming at a notoriously Dickensian cheese factory for a story about migrant women workers. We talked our way in there on the basis of doing a story about the factory. Of course in that situation you delay the real interview until the very last minute, so you go around the factory, get all the shots of the women working standing up when they could have been sitting down, and carrying big boxes of cheese over slimy floors.

The man who owned the factory thought this was the best thing that had ever happened to him because he was going to get all this publicity on national television. And he took us out to lunch, and gave us the five-star treatment, you know, and thought I was his brother, and there was going to come the inevitable moment of deep and thorough-going betrayal—from his point of view anyway.

From my point of view, I thought he had a really substantive case to answer in terms of the way he was treating his workforce, but I also had to be prepared for the fact that he'd bolt when he realised what was happening and there was no way apart from having a firm response ready.

So I said to him—and this was a real dry-throat breathless sort of anxiety thing because I was looking him right in the eye—I mean if you're going to stab anybody, you know, it takes extra guts to do it right in the front.

And I said, 'Tell me what section of what award entitles you to get these women to clean your Rolls-Royce at lunch time.'

Which I thought set the tone of the interview fairly clearly, and he tried to get out of the chair and I mean that would have had a certain dramatic appeal, except we hadn't really got the interview going. And what could I do about it? Nothing. Except to wag my finger at him and say very sternly, 'Why don't you just sit there and answer the questions?' Which is something I've never done ever before or since, and it worked. And he sat there ... like a little boy, and in the end, on the first cut of the documentary I didn't run terribly much of him because I thought he almost looked like a figure of the underdog, but then others thought I was being a bit too sensitive.

But that's the great occasion when I've really choked, and had to say to myself, come on, let's get real, let's get on with it (personal interview with Paul Lyneham).

DO TRY the 'how does it feel' question— sparingly

This question is overdone by the media, appears to be asking the obvious, and is the one question the public complains that it hears far too often. The journalist who asks the champion swimmer, 'How does it feel to have made the Olympic team?' does not expect them to say, 'It feels terrible.' Put more thought into this question if you want to use it. You could ask the swimmer: 'What was the best feeling—knowing you had made the Olympic team, or that you had broken the world record?'

Despite its overuse, the 'How does it feel?' question will almost always work in a positive situation, as with the swimmer. However, caution must be used if you decide to ask this question in less happy circumstances. For instance, the television journalist who asks recently bereaved parents: 'How does it feel to know you will never see your child again?' cannot expect them to be very forthcoming.

This sort of question can also be used as an aggressive device, but you must be prepared to hold your ground if the interviewee becomes defensive.

Example

For instance, with the bank official you could try:

Q: How does it feel to have the fate of the staff in this region in your hands?

However, don't be surprised if the official becomes less than helpful after you ask this.

DO TRY projection

To soften the difficult question, or to reduce hostility in the interview, journalists often project accusations to a third party—'some people might say' or 'your critics might ask'. The most famous example of using this technique—and seeing it go wrong—is the much-repeated 1981 interview between British Prime Minister

Margaret Thatcher and George Negus (who was a journalist for Channel 9's *60 Minutes* at the time).

> GN: Why do people stop us in the street almost and tell us that Margaret Thatcher isn't just inflexible, she's not just single-minded, on occasions she's just plain pig headed and won't be told by anyone?
> MT: Would you tell me who has stopped you in the street and said that?
> GN: Ordinary Britons.
> MT: Where?
> GN: In conversation, in pubs . . .
> MT (Interrupting): I thought you'd just come from Belize.
> GN: Oh, it's not the first time we've been here.
> MT: Will you tell me who and where and when?
> GN: Ordinary Britons in restaurants and cabs.
> MT: How many?
> GN: I would say at least one in two.
> MT: I'm sorry, it's an expression that I've never heard . . . tell me who has said it to you, when and where? (Little 1994: 23–4).

Of course, Negus couldn't. While this exchange was described as 'good television', it should serve as a warning if you plan to make use of the projection technique.

DO TRY the 'dumb' or innocent question

Asking the innocent or 'dumb' question such as 'I don't really understand this. Could you explain it to me?' can work very well, particularly in getting the interviewee to explain something in simpler terms more suited for the publication or broadcast. It is also a useful device to get the interviewee to reveal more information.

Example

With the bank official, you could ask:

Q: I'm sorry, I don't quite understand. Could you explain how you decide whether a branch is viable?

However, the journalist at an international press conference following a major basketball tournament took this technique a little bit too far when he asked: 'Could you tell me please why you get two points when you score a goal?'

DO TRY the leading question

This technique is used as a way of getting the interviewee to use your words in their answer. It might work if the interviewee agrees with what you are saying, but otherwise it is rare that your lead will be used.

Example

For instance, it is unlikely the interviewee will use any of the words from the following question, as they would not want to repeat any negative ideas.

Q: Could this tour be seen as just another way of penalising people for living outside metropolitan centres?

However, if you asked:

Q: Is this tour one way of ensuring customers have the services they require?

The interviewee may well answer:

A: Yes, this is the major way we ensure regional customers have the services they require.

DO TRY the trick question

Sometimes a question can be worded in such a way that the interviewee will be trapped if they attempt to answer it. This technique is generally used with those who are trained in dealing with the media and either is left unanswered, or the answer could be that they have recognised the trick. It might work, but it is rare when it does.

Example

Q: Don't you feel it is unfair to look at reducing services in this region?

Whichever way the bank official answers—yes or no—it will be a confirmation that services are being reduced, so a savvy interviewee would deflect this question.

DO TRY

- Repeating or rephrasing questions
- Posing a hypothetical question
- Playing the devil's advocate
- The tough question

DO TRY

- The 'how does it feel' question—sparingly
- Projection
- The 'dumb' or innocent question
- The leading question
- The trick question

DON'T ASK double- or triple-barrelled questions

Questions that are 'two in one' or even 'three in one' are confusing for even the best and most practised interviewees. If a journalist asks a long triple-barrelled question, the interviewee would be likely to choose either the easiest question of the three or the last question. Some interviewees are so proficient at interviews that they will answer all three, but this sort of ability is rare.

Example

Don't ask the bank official:

Q: Do you plan to close bank branches as a result of this tour, and will this be the first time you have conducted a tour such as this?

It would be an unusually rare and forthcoming interviewee who would answer the first question when given the option.

DON'T ASK the 'tell me all about yourself' question—unless specific

This is an incredibly lazy question and everyone knows it, even someone who is rarely interviewed. One journalist asked this exact question at the start of an interview with a university professor. The professor handed him a CV and told him to come back when he had some 'real' questions to ask.

Another example involved a press conference with actor Robert Carlyle and a group of international journalists.

He seemed to be warming up and ready to talk about his recent big life shock—a newspaper tracking down the mother he hadn't seen for thirty years since she walked out on him when he was a small boy—when a German journalist took the floor. 'Robert,' he said, 'please, I have never heard of you before. Tell me about what other things you have done' (Williams 1997: 14).

Sometimes the 'tell me about yourself' question is used in feature interviews, but usually in reference to a more specific timeframe or situation such as, 'Tell me what it was like when you heard about your father's death', or 'Tell me all about yourself when you decided to travel to India'.

DON'T ASK

- Double- or triple-barrelled questions
- The 'tell me all about yourself' question—unless in relation to a specific event or time

DO KEEP in focus and in control

One of the most important elements of an interview, and often the most difficult, is maintaining control. Some journalists will rise to the bait and start verbal sparring with the interviewee. All this does is get the interviewee off the hook, while the journalist loses control, their cool and—in the case of broadcast journalists—the respect of the audience.

In her interview with media tycoon Rupert Murdoch, Jana Wendt admirably maintained her cool after some very personal barbs were sent her way. She kept the focus and continued with the interview despite several attempts of provocation. The interview was primarily about Murdoch's attempts to set up a Super League. In the following segment Murdoch appears to be trying to take control of the interview by posing a question to Wendt, and then attempts to bait her about 'astronomical salaries'. Wendt continues with her line of questioning, and eventually Murdoch, who had been denying the large offers of money, agrees with Wendt's original statement.

RM: Why were they so loyal to us?

JW: Money?

RM: No. They get money—they were offered other money.

JW: They were offered astronomical amounts of money by you.

RM: Well, not by your standards. (smiles)

JW: Astronomical amounts of money by any standards. Multiples of their salaries previously.

RM: No, I don't know about that. It depends who and what the bidding was, and so on. Some, sure, I mean some were going to be paid properly (Channel 7 1996).

Above all—try to avoid the obvious. For instance, the journalist who asked the two members of the popular singing group *sister2sister* 'How did you meet?' should probably go back to the drawing board.

REFERENCES

Biagi, S. 1986, *Interviews that Work: A Practical Guide for Journalists*, Wadsworth, Belmont, CA

Channel 7 9 April 1996, interview by Jana Wendt with Rupert Murdoch, *Witness*, Sydney, NSW

Little, J. 1994, *Inside 60 Minutes*, Allen & Unwin, Sydney, NSW

Williams, S. 23 April 1997, 'Interviews: the stupid in pursuit of the irrelevant', *The Australian*, p. 14

6 PRINT INTERVIEWS

> 'Well then, just tell me about your wedding night.'
>
> A long silence. Then a woman said, 'It was seven minutes.'
>
> Another exclaimed, 'Seven minutes?'
>
> At that point, I had no idea what they were talking about, but for the next two hours the group had an enthusiastic discussion. I didn't have to ask another question (Lobsenz 2009: 2).

The above conversation emerged when Lobsenz was asked to write an article for a bridal magazine concerning recently married couples and their thoughts on sex. Lobsenz provides this example of an interview to highlight the problem with sensitive topics that may yield cryptic responses or no responses at all and therefore may need a challenging or confrontational approach (Lobsenz 2009: 2). He initially wasn't able to extract any useful information.

If you are finding that anecdotal material is proving problematic (that is, the interviewee either has difficulty remembering details or can't think of anything to say) then use questions structured in such a way that these details can be elicited. For example, ask, 'What happened to you at that point?' or, 'And then what did you say?' or, 'What made you decide to do that?' (Lobsenz 2009: 2). Lobsenz encourages the interviewer to be persistent as he finds eventually there will be worthwhile responses.

Andrea Carson, former industrial reporter for Melbourne's *Age*, says she still uses the two pieces of advice she was given about interviewing when she first started working as a print journalist—to recheck details such as title and spelling of name, and to ask whether the interviewee wanted to add anything that hadn't been covered. 'The first piece of advice avoided a lot of errors, and the second often resulted in a really good angle coming up at the end of the interview, with them talking about an area I had not thought to ask about' (personal interview with Andrea Carson).

Print news interviews can be divided into two major categories: hard news (which is usually spot news or news of the day and heavily fact-reliant); and soft news (which is timeless material featuring people, celebrities or issues). There are also many variations within these categories that govern the length of the interview and the techniques used. The hard news interview could be seeking the latest facts for anything from a three-paragraph news brief about a road accident to a major cover story exposing corruption. The soft news interview focuses on the human interest angles (or the emotions), and is very often for a personality piece (a feature story about a person).

The hard news brief requires the journalist to concentrate on the basic questions (Who, What, When and Where) and generally is about 'who said what' or 'who did what'. The investigative story also seeks these basic facts, but must extend the interview to obtain comment and opinion—aiming to discover the 'Why' and 'How' of the issue. While also seeking facts and quotes, the personality piece concentrates on 'softer' angles designed to appeal to the emotions.

Kerry O'Brien says when you're doing a hard news interview the questions are fairly self-evident, but you should 'cast your net' further with less obvious questions in feature interviews.

If it's a road accident: What were the conditions? What caused it? What was the state of the road? Was the driver DUI [driving under the influence]? Those things are obvious. However, when I was doing features for newspapers you would tend to cast your net a bit. You could be somewhat more conversational in the way you put the questions. As a newspaper journalist I've got no doubt I was much less disciplined as an interviewer than I am now. Provided the person on the other side of the desk was willing, you could sit for an hour doing what you might have 15 minutes to do, or 10 minutes to do in television, and then you could go back at your own pace and distil it all down and work it all through (personal interview with Kerry O'Brien).

There is no set formula for conducting any of these interviews, but there are some essential steps that should be carried out before, during and after the exchange. To demonstrate these steps we use an interview with Jon Coyne, a bank official conducting a tour of small country branches, as an example. The first interview is a hard news piece and incorporates interviewing for fact and opinion, while the second interview is a feature profile piece on the bank official.

Each case study details sixteen essential steps for a print interview. Chapters 2 and 3 of this book provide full details about these steps.

CASE STUDY 1: Hard news interview for fact and opinion—sixteen key steps

While the following case study includes steps for conducting a hard news interview, the list below, and its order of presentation, is not prescriptive. Every interview you conduct will be different and should be treated as such.

1 Arrange an interview time and place
2 Do your research
3 Organise your questions or keywords
4 Organise your notepad and equipment
5 Arrive at the interview early
6 Get set up and check your equipment again
7 Ask your icebreaker question
8 Explain the purpose of the interview
9 Ask your first interview question
10 Ask the What, When, Where and Who questions
11 Ask the comment or opinion questions
12 *Listen* to the answers
13 Ask the 'who cares' or 'who will be affected' question
14 Follow up with the challenge or investigative question
15 Ask if there's anything they would like to add before you finish, and if the interviewee has time
16 Check your notes.

Don't forget to thank the interviewee for their valuable time after you have completed these steps.

Sixteen key steps in detail

1 **Arrange an interview time and place.** The venue can play a major role in the success or otherwise of an interview. Choosing a quiet spot is particularly important for a broadcast interview that is being recorded. A quiet spot is also helpful for a print interview as it can be difficult to concentrate and decipher your notes on a busy thoroughfare or in a bustling café. Choosing a suitable time can also be important, particularly with busy interviewees. If you choose a time on the hour—such as 4 pm—the interviewee may well perceive it as an open-ended slot (at least for an hour anyway), and be unwilling to commit to this amount of time. However, if you choose 3.45 pm, or even 3.30 pm, it appears as though you have confined the interview to a shorter time—between fifteen and thirty minutes respectively. This first step should also be the time when you introduce yourself and your organisation, and ensure that the interviewee knows the interview will be on the record and for publication. Confirm all arrangements (date, time and place) at the end of this step.

2 **Do your research.** Even if you only have a short time before the interview, use it for research. The more you can find out about the person and the issue, the better the interview result. Author and journalist Shirley Biagi believes 'the ideal situation is to have weeks for research before an interview and weeks to write the story afterward. But this is a fantasy. Reporters usually write an interview story the day they do the interview' (Biagi 1986: 3).

3 **Organise your questions or keywords.** Actually writing down your questions will help

you focus your attention on the issue or person. They could be written on one page of your notepad. Before you organise your questions you should summarise the purpose or 'angle' of your interview. If you cannot do this in less than thirty words, it's back to the drawing board. You should have a clear and concise idea of what you want from the interview, but don't be afraid to deviate if new angles appear.

4 **Organise your notepad and equipment.** There's nothing more embarrassing than having your one and only pen run out halfway through an interview. Of course any equipment used in the print interview—probably a recording device (and perhaps a camera for photographs)—should be checked and rechecked before an interview.

5 **Arrive at the interview early.** Early is good—but no more than about five minutes. If you arrive much earlier than that it puts pressure on the interviewee to finish what they are doing sooner than they had planned, and your super-punctuality might not be appreciated.

6 **Get set up and check your equipment again.** In these few minutes before the interview get set up and comfortable. If the interviewee is not conversant with media interviews, you might want to wait until you have progressed through your icebreaker before you bring out any recording devices (or even your notepad).

7 **Ask your icebreaker question.** This is where your research is essential in providing an area of interest to use for the icebreaker. If you do not have the luxury of this preparation, you could comment on the surroundings or something in the news that day. If all else fails, talk about the weather.

8 **Explain the purpose of the interview.** Start your interview by explaining what you are hoping to achieve, and where and when the story is likely to be used. Do not give a guarantee that it will be used in the next edition of the newspaper as a major story may break, pushing yours out.

9 **Ask your first question.** With print interviews you usually have the time to ask your easy questions first, working up to the 'tough' questions or 'bombs'. The correct title and spelling of the interviewee's name should be number 1 on your list. Remember: don't assume anything. Even if your interviewee's name is 'Jon Coyne', you cannot assume the usual spelling of these names. 'Jon' could be spelt 'John', 'Jonn' or 'Johnn'. At this point don't forget to request their preferred title.

TIP

Please do not take this advice too literally—some cadet journalists have even asked prime ministers to spell their names!

---

10 **Ask the What, When, Where and Who questions.** While the subject of the interview is generally the 'Who', quite often they are involved with others in the context of the story. In this case you would need to clarify which bank branches were to be included in the audit and the customers who could be affected. Jon Coyne, the bank staff and the customers are the 'Who' in this story.

11 **Ask the comment (How) or opinion (Why) questions.** In this story the 'Why' is particularly critical. You should ask questions such as: 'Why is the audit being conducted in this region?', 'Why

have these particular branches been chosen?' and 'How will this affect farmers in the region?'

12 **Listen.** Definitely worth a section on its own. It should be understood that you are observing and listening throughout the whole interview— listening to answers and ensuring that the interviewee's body language is in sync with their verbal responses. Listening is critical, and in fact may produce totally unexpected results. If an answer deviates from your list of questions make sure you note it down, together with a small question or keyword nearby to make sense of the answer. For example, on checking your notes to write the story you may find the answer: 'Definitely, that's what we intend to do.' You know it's critical because you've put a star beside it, but you can't recall the question that prompted the response.

13 **Ask the 'who cares' or 'who will be affected' question.** This is a critical question and could determine the prominence of the story when published. For instance if, through questioning, you were able to find out that the audit was going to result in a reduction of jobs and services, it may well make page 1 of the newspaper. This is because there is a large group of people 'who care' and will be affected by, or interested in, this story. Generally the larger the group, the more prominent the story (in terms of placement and size). So any story that the editor believes has a high percentage of readers 'who care' will be placed in a prominent position, such as pages 1 or 3, and may fill the whole page. Those judged to have a smaller interested reader-ship will take up less space and may be relegated to the back pages.

14 **Follow up with the challenge or investigative question.** Time for the 'bomb' or tough question. In this particular interview the tough question may well be the same as the 'who cares' question. This should be left until the end of the interview. If the interviewee handles this question well, then continue with some softer questions before dropping another 'bomb'. If you don't get suitable answers—ones that you can easily understand, or ones that your readers will easily understand—ask again. This applies to all your questions.

15 **The end of the interview often is the source of a new angle.** Ask if there is anything they want to add. This might produce an angle that has not occurred to you.

16 **Check your notes.** If you have covered all the areas you had planned in your interview, now is the time to check through your notes. Explain to the interviewee that you are checking to ensure you have all the information you need. Most interviewees would prefer to spend a couple of minutes at the end of the interview while you check your notes, rather than receive a number of follow-up telephone calls or emails chasing missed information. Check any answers you don't fully understand. Though you want to avoid any further imposition on the interviewee's time, ensure that you have full contact details before you leave the interview. Telephone numbers for work and home, a mobile number, email address and fax number can be lifesavers. Don't hesitate to check facts if you are unsure— the interviewee would undoubtedly prefer you to impose on their time than see mistakes printed in the newspaper the next day.

TIP

In Step 16 make sure you have answers to the five Ws and one H. If it helps, list these six essential questions in your notepad so it is easy to check at the end (see below).

Who: Jon Coyne, Title: Bank Audit Manager, Bankco
What: Full audit of bank branches
When: At the start of the new financial year
Where: Regional branches
Why: To assess the viability of the branches ...
How: A full audit incorporating staff, services ...

Thank the interviewee for their valuable time.

CASE STUDY 2: Soft news feature interview for a personality piece—sixteen key steps

The bank audit manager for Bankco, Jon Coyne, is about to retire after 40 years of service with the same bank. While the first seven steps for a feature interview are relatively similar to those for a news interview, you are seeking different information. As Len Granato notes in *Newspaper Feature Writing*: 'a human-interest feature story is a creative, sometimes subjective, article designed primarily to entertain and only secondarily to inform ... they are anchored in the human emotions—joy, tragedy, humour, love, hate, sorrow, jealousy' (1997: 3). You will generally have more time in a feature interview to elicit information that should include facts, quotes, anecdotes and description.

Every interview is different and should be treated as such. The following sixteen steps are suggestions for what may be covered in a print feature interview.

However, Steps 3, 4, 5, 6 and 7 are almost identical in every interview. They have been included here as a reminder.

1 Arrange a couple of interview times
2 Do your research
3 Organise your questions or keywords
4 Organise your notepad and equipment
5 Arrive at the interview early
6 Get set up and check your equipment again
7 Ask your icebreaker question
8 Observe your interviewee and their surroundings
9 Ask your first interview question
10 Don't forget to *listen*
11 Ask the 'easy' questions first
12 Look for off-beat questions
13 Make time to get anecdotes
14 Gather essential background
15 Ask if there's anything they would like to add before you finish, and if the interviewee has time
16 Check your notes.

Sixteen key steps in detail

1 **Arrange a couple of interview times.** The ideal when interviewing someone for a feature story is to be able to interview them at least twice—preferably face to face both times and in different locations. More often now an interview is first performed by email then followed up face to face. A feature story should cover the public and private persona of the interviewee, and the separate locations can aid in this endeavour. If the story is primarily about their work, hobby, art or sport, the first interview should be conducted

where they are involved in these pursuits. In this way you can get a feel for their 'job', their surrounds and how they interact with others. It would be ideal to catch the person at home for the second interview, but if this is not possible try to interview them in a 'neutral' location such as a not-too-noisy café away from other interruptions. Confirm any arrangements. Obviously you will need to explain the reason you require the interview(s) and where and when it is likely to be published. As with your hard news story, don't give cast-iron guarantees.

2 **Do your research.** It would be very rare not to have advance notice of print feature interviews. With some celebrities and sports stars you will probably have to organise the interview months in advance. This is good! Use this time to dig hard for everything you can about the interviewee. Celebrities and sports stars tend to get a little jaded because of the number of interviews they conduct, so it is nice if you can surprise them with a new question or information about an interest of theirs that is not widely known. Use primary and secondary sources for your information. Primary sources are other people who can give you reliable information about your interviewee and can include their friends, family, colleagues, team members and employees. Make sure you talk to other primary sources before you do your main interviews. Sometimes your own family, friends and colleagues may also be good sources of information about your interviewee. Secondary sources consist of information produced by others—newspaper clippings, magazine articles, Internet sites, journals, books and newsletters are just some.

3 **Organise your questions or keywords.** Because a feature story will generally be far longer than a news story, you will need to collect more information in your interview(s). This means longer interviews if you have a number of questions and key areas to cover. Even though this is not a news story, it is still helpful to summarise the expected angle or theme before organising the questions or keywords. Write this down in less than 30 words, but don't be concerned if the theme changes after the interview(s).

The following three steps are the same as those used in the hard news interview.

4 **Organise your notepad and equipment.**
5 **Arrive at the interview early.**
6 **Get set up and check your equipment again.**
7 **Ask your icebreaker question.** Your research will probably be essential in providing an icebreaker, but don't discount using additional on-the-spot observations to help establish a rapport. For instance, if you are interviewing someone at their home, your observations will be extremely useful to get the conversation going. Photographs, pets, books, trophies and their music collection are obvious clues.
8 **Observe your interviewee and their surroundings.** Your observations should provide valuable additions to your final story. Feature stories should consist of three main elements: facts, quotes and anecdotes. However, many feature writers believe a fourth element—description—should be included as an essential. Len Granato points out that:

just as people have individual ways of speaking, they have individual ways of looking and acting. They assert their individuality by how they dress, how they wear their hair . . . how they relate to other people, how they feel about things, how they furnish and decorate their personal space. Good description conveys people's images and their personalities (1997: 81).

However, Granato goes on to warn that you 'should never try to tell the reader what to think about anything. Your job is not to instruct the reader but to provide observations that allow the reader to make his or her own interpretations and draw his or her own conclusions' (1997: 81).

The interviewee's surroundings should also be included, whether it is at a home, office, studio or favourite coffee shop. Granato points out that you need to 'be selective. Since you can't describe everything, select aspects that will tell the reader something about the source: the photographs of the spouse on the desk, the ship in a bottle on the bookcase, the best actress award on the piano' (1997: 82).

9 **Ask your first interview question.** With feature interviews it does not hurt to confirm the correct title and spelling of the interviewee's name first. Remember: don't assume anything. As with the news interview, please don't ask for the spelling of the person's name or their title if they are well known.

10 **Don't forget to listen.** It should be understood that listening, and observing, is essential in any interview. Of all the techniques a journalist can use, most agree that listening is the key to interviewing success.

11 **Ask the 'easy' questions first.** In the case of the feature interview this will depend to a large extent on your interviewee. If it is someone familiar with being interviewed, spend less time at this stage. However, others may be put at ease by a slower start. You will need fact for your story, so collect that first. Questions for Jon Coyne could include: 'Where were you born?', 'Where did you grow up?', 'What was your first job?', 'What is your job now?', 'What are your hobbies?', 'How many children do you have?', 'How many grandchildren do you have?' and so on.

12 **Look for off-beat questions.** You don't want to overload your story with quotes, but you do want to feature some of the interviewee's thoughts and opinions. Jon Coyne could be asked: 'Did you always enjoy your work?', 'Have you had time to enjoy your hobbies and family?', 'What do you think about the banking system of today?' ABC's Kerry O'Brien says you should be looking for the off-beat questions:

> These are the questions that are going to give people that little extra insight into the person you're interviewing that they might not other-wise get, or that they won't get if you just ask the predictable. Always be looking for those questions that other journalists are not going to think of (personal interview with Kerry O'Brien).

For instance, you could ask Jon Coyne: Did you dream of being a fireman when you were a child?

13 **Make time to get anecdotes.** Anecdotes are the lifeblood of a feature story. They are basically small stories explaining a situation—usually humorous.

They give a story vitality, but are quite difficult to elicit. As you are collecting your facts and quotes, there will invariably be opportunities to ask for anecdotes. Don't be too general when asking for these 'stories'. For instance, asking 'What was the best moment of your career?' is a little general and may prove difficult for the interviewee. However, when talking to Jon Coyne about his first job, you may well ask, 'What was your first day like?' or 'What was the worst moment/best moment?' When talking about his family, Jon may well tell you that he followed his father's footsteps into banking. He might have a memory of going in and watching his father at work that would make a great anecdote. This step may take quite a while, and may happen progressively throughout the interview when you are talking about certain topics. You may also elicit anecdotes about your subject from other primary sources such as family and friends.

14 **Gather essential background.** You will need to find out more about key people in Jon's life, for instance, his father and his wife. This is also the time to get background on the organisation Jon is leaving if this hasn't come up earlier in the interview.

15 **Ask if the interviewee has anything to add that hasn't been covered.**

16 **Check your notes.** With a feature interview you sometimes get the most interesting information at the end when the interviewee relaxes. Check your notes and ask for clarification on any unclear information. You may also have to ask extra questions to elicit anecdotes if you feel you haven't got enough 'colour' in the story. Ensure you have contact details for any follow-up questions and any other sources.

Don't forget to thank the interviewee for all their valuable time. It is important to acknowledge that the interviewee is being generous with their time and in sharing their story with you. Not only have they given you their story but also you might need to interview them at a later date, so it is always a good policy to finish on a positive note.

REFERENCES

Biagi, S. 1986, *Interviews that Work: A Practical Guide for Journalists*, Wadsworth, Belmont, CA

Granato, L. 1997, *Newspaper Feature Writing*, Deakin University Press, Geelong, Vic

Lobsenz, N. 1 May 2009, 'The most common interview problems: and how to get around them', *The Writer*, vol. 122, no. 5, pp. 32-3, http://www.writermag.com; Australian/ New Zealand Reference Centre database, Accession no. 37365139, pp. 1-2, accessed 21 January 2010

7 BROADCAST INTERVIEWS

For all interviewers one of the golden rules of interviewing is to always be prepared, especially for the unexpected. In other words, it is helpful for an interviewer to consider the possible responses to any given question and to devise follow-up questions, given a particular response. Some of the most experienced interviewers find that a particular reaction throws them off track—what is then important is the recovery.

> Andrew Denton: You saw him decline and die from that. You are somebody who lives in your mind and you saw the man you love lose his. That must have had a powerful impact on you.
>
> Helen Thomas: Oh yes but I more powerful was my family helped me. I never put him in [a] home or ...
>
> AD: Yes, that is remarkable. Your sister in particular took him in, is that right?
>
> HT: No. This is the moment you wanted. *(Thomas gets visibly upset at this point.)*

> AD: No, not all, and if you'd rather I didn't.
>
> HT: I don't want to sit around and to apologise for my life.
>
> AD: I don't want you to apologise for your life. Far from it. I'm ... what we're talking about here is what's happened in your life and what ...
>
> HT: What do you think happens, for God's sakes? You see someone deteriorate before your eyes.
>
> AD: I think we just stop for the minute. And I apologise.
>
> HT: It's not your fault.
>
> AD: Well I—it is to a certain extent. I didn't realise that you felt that strongly. I thought we had, it was clear that these sorts of things were going to be talked about.
>
> HT: No, my reaction surprises me.
>
> *(Laughter)*
>
> AD: Yeah, and look, I'm genuinely sorry because that was not. I try to be very upfront.
>
> HT: It's not you, it's not your fault.
>
> *(Interview resumes after a visible pause in recording.)*
>
> AD: What I'm asking about is how you move on from that.
>
> HT: It's a loss. How do you, how does anyone do it? You just pass through, go on living, that's all. I mean, it isn't something like meeting some traumatic black grim reaper and then suddenly, you know, you overcome it. You just live, that's all. (Excerpt from *Enough Rope*, ABC 2008).

During this interview, Helen Thomas (a White House press correspondent) was questioned about her husband, Douglas, who died of Alzheimer's disease. Thomas surprised both herself and Denton with her emotional reaction to the question about her sister caring for her husband, saying 'No. This is the moment you wanted', as well as revealing her scepticism of Denton's motive for asking this question (ABC 2008: 9). Denton in response indicated that he didn't want to upset Thomas and also offers to avoid the subject of Thomas's husband, though this line of questioning had been agreed on earlier.

Denton, in his recovery, apologises and freely admits Thomas's response is partly his fault, stating, 'I didn't realise that you felt that strongly. I thought we had, it was clear that these sorts of things were going to be talked about' (ABC 2008: 9). In addition to stating he thought he had Thomas's permission to discuss her husband's illness, he also reinforces that his intent was not to sensationalise the outcome of the interview but to maintain an honest and open approach when he says, 'I try to be very upfront' (ABC 2008: 9).

Denton's reaction to Thomas's emotional responses is clearly evidence of an interviewer who is actively listening. But more than that, he is adjusting the course of the interview as he proceeds to ensure Thomas feels comfortable with the direction it is taking while still ensuring it is both interesting and revealing.

RADIO INTERVIEWS

'If you want to learn how to interview go and talk to a bunch of kids, because kids give you honest answers and they teach you the most fundamental lesson in radio interviewing and that is: never ask a question to which the answer is "yes" or "no"' (personal interview with Al Morrison).

Radio New Zealand's political editor Al Morrison has been a working journalist all his life and has moved from print journalism to broadcast journalism. So what's the difference? He says that broadcast interviewing is both different from, and the same as, print interviewing. In many ways the same principles of basic, quality journalism apply in broadcast interviewing—

asking the right questions, listening and thinking about what it is the public wants to know. But there are differences, too. The big difference, he says, is that 'what you're really aiming for in broadcast interviews is tape'—in other words, usable video or audio recordings. In television interviews, the difference is both the pictures and the sound.

Another important difference relating to live formats is that you as the reporter are likely to be seen as well as heard in broadcast interviews. Your questions may be broadcast during a radio interview, and you may be seen and heard during television interviews. In print journalism you may get away with the odd witless question because readers seldom see what was asked; they see only the answers in an edited format within the text of the story. In radio and television there is no place for a dumb question because you may be heard and seen asking it.

THE TYRANNY OF TIME

The tyranny of time nags at broadcast journalists. Kerry O'Brien agrees, and says if you're doing live interviews for television, or live interviews for radio, you've got the tyranny of time—'the tyranny of the clock ticking'.

And it seems to tick awfully fast when you're in a television studio. Which is why when you get to a certain level of interviewing you will find you're confronted by decisions on the run—whether you really should be interjecting at this point, and at what point you go too far in your interjection, and simply having made your point to the audience, move on. These things can be matters of very fine balance (personal interview with Kerry O'Brien).

But it is not only the unremitting nature of deadlines that radio and television journalists have to worry about. They often have to try to make stories as timeless as possible. Time, intimacy and intensity are all accentuated in broadcast interviews. Radio reporters have to cope with reading, writing and creating hourly news bulletins, and perhaps even contributing longer pieces to current affairs stories. Different program formats also require stories of different length and style.

Television is also about immediacy and reporter involvement. Reporters must quickly learn to go to air live in front of the camera and not make a fool of themselves. Kerry O'Brien points out that 'panic gets you nowhere'. He says it can help to 'force yourself to take five minutes out between when you get your assignment, and when you actually have to do it, to go and look out a window and try and collect your thoughts'.

> If you do feel a sense of panic, or think 'God, what am I going to do?', then you just remind yourself that it's all going to be over in a short space of time anyway, and at some point in the not too distant future it will have become a dim memory. In the meantime you're just going to get through it with as much dignity as you can muster (personal interview with Kerry O'Brien).

Very often the reporter can be the one being interviewed by an anchor or program host, so the journalist must know as much about being an interviewee as being an interviewer. Carel Pedre, a radio and television presenter based at Haiti, found himself in precisely that situation on 13 January 2010 when his role was reversed because usual news delivery operations had been affected by the earthquake. Instead he used Skype to provide information about the crisis as it unfolded to CBS News and other news agencies (Paul 2010: 1–2).

Reporters also need to know about the different sorts of interviews conducted on radio and television and to adapt their interviewing styles accordingly. The different types of

interview relate to the use of recording devices in radio reporting and audiovisual recordings in television journalism. The
highly visual nature of television interviewing means that if
there are no pictures, there is no story. Broadcast reporters have
to be pushy. At press conferences and out on location they
need their microphones and cameras to be well positioned so
that they can collect good-quality audio and visuals.

SKYPE

Skype, a software application, uses voice over Internet protocol
(VoIP) and web camera technology whereby voice signals are
changed into data streams that are delivered by the Internet
and changed back to audio by the user's computer receiving
these signals. Skype communications use a P2P (peer to peer)
model; that is, the communications are direct; it is essentially
one computer speaking to another. This technology encourages
increased contact on a work and personal basis that tends to
make it preferable to email.

Freelance journalist Kelly James-Enger writes in her article
'The cost-conscious freelancer' that the use of Skype for international communications has a number of economic advantages
compared to landline telephone use, in that 'Skype to Skype is
free' (Sam Greengard quoted in James–Enger 2009:1) and Skype
to a landline or mobile phone incurs a minimal fee. Skype has
been released for both the Apple iPhone and the BlackBerry, the
latter of which doesn't need Wi-Fi to connect, just a BlackBerry
data (calling) plan.

With Skype, aside from the application of voice calls there
are also the options of Instant Messaging (IM) and conference
calls. However, what has emerged with the use of Skype technology is journalists' use of this medium to report the news and
to connect to any interviewee at any given location, worldwide.
As part of the preparation for an interview Skype is particularly

'good for setting up interviews and informal discussions' (Sam Greengard quoted in James-Enger 2009: 1).

Although the sound and visual aspects are questionable regarding quality, the ease of access to and economics of Skype have established its use as a globally recognised tool for journalists and broadcast networks. A good example of Skype's application can be seen regularly on the Ten television network's show *Oprah*, where Skype is used as part of the interviewing process to speak to interviewees on site. Just one example was the Skype interview with three students immediately after an extensive makeover of their dormitory room (broadcast on 13 April 2009, USA).

THE PODCAST NETWORK

We are living in an age where there are sophisticated technological broadcast alternatives. In 2005, the Podcast Network (TPN) commenced broadcasting. Based in Melbourne, TPN is an Australian podcasting business which in 2005 reached an audience in excess of 250,000 from '150 countries' with a comprehensive range of programs covering aspects of business management, technology, movies, health and fitness through to educational shows that for example discuss Napoleon Bonaparte (Simons 2007: 78; TPN 2007).

While TPN represents competition for radio broadcasters, again the point must be made as with other independent content makers—for instance, stand-alone journalists within the online environment—that quality journalism sustains and endures. 'The goal of TPN is to bring together talented and committed podcasters from around the world to produce high quality programming for a global audience . . . Some of our podcasters are making hundreds and even thousands of dollars a month from sponsorship deals but it isn't about the money. It's about providing bloody good stuff for your ears and eyes and brains. If we can do that well enough, we believe the rest will follow' (The Podcast Network 2007).

TPN has been profitable and, at the close of 2006, the network's best show was a 'news program "G'day world", put together by Duncan Riley—a well-known personality in the Internet-media world but virtually unknown in the mainstream media. His first show for 2007 covered everything from Federal Health Minister Tony Abbott's intervention in the abortion debate to a review of the new James Bond movie *Casino Royale*' (Simons 2007: 78).

Podcasting is an immediate form of broadcasting that requires the podcaster to be fully prepared and conversant with the subject of choice and aware of the visual impression they can create and leave with the audience.

RECORDING DEVICES

In radio interviews 'while you're interviewing you not only have to listen to the content of the answer, you have to listen to it for the ten-, fifteen-, thirty-second or even minute section that really encapsulates what the person is trying to say, not just the dramatic bit but the bit that fairly captures what the person is trying to say' (personal interview with Al Morrison). This section or 'grab' can sometimes be as short as three to five seconds in a radio news bulletin.

Grabs comes in different types. Short snips of audio are played in a story as part of the broadcast item. These cuts or 'grabs' are usually of people talking, although when New Zealand's Mount Ruapehu volcano erupted, audio of the noise of the eruption with rocks, steam and lava belching out of the volcano lake was broadcast. There are four categories of recorded material: actualities, questions and answers, voicers and wraps.

Actualities

Actualities are basic kinds of recordings. They allow listeners a chance to hear voices of real people, such as eyewitnesses to US President Barack Obama's inauguration, who talk naturally and convey the excitement, fear or sadness and sense of being there. Very often they do not speak grammatically, may use colloquial language and do not finish their sentences. Once you have collected the recordings from an eyewitness to an event like a tsunami, how do you select the actuality you want? Generally it is when the newsmaker says something in a much clearer, or more emotive, way than the journalist ever could. Actualities can include eyewitness reports, expert knowledge from the police, for example, comments by staff of the Bureau of Meteorology, and subjective comments from news sources about their feelings and beliefs.

Questions and answers

Q and As are where the question is either heard on radio or seen being asked and heard on television. Radio and television interviews that feature questions and answers can be conducted in the studio live. Other broadcast interviews are conducted on the telephone, or at a press conference with other reporters present, as well as face to face with a news-maker. These days there are many options available for the face-to-face interview, such as Skype.

Voicers

Many voicers are written out in advance but usually on the run—on a scrap of paper, in a field notepad or an address book—or in the car. Voicers are sometimes referred to in television as part of the 'stand-up syndrome' by which reporters stand in front of the camera and become the news-maker and can be an alternative when there is no news-maker present, such as describing a fire or Mount Ruapehu erupting, before officials or survivors can be found for interviews. They can supplement Q and As and actualities.

Wraps

Wraps are like a broadcast sandwich, with one layer of a voicer, then a layer of actuality and then a voicer again. First the reporter's voice is heard, then the news-maker is heard with the reporter being heard again in conclusion.

The reporter wraps the story around the actuality, and usually it becomes a self-contained story. For example:

Reporter: Mount Ruapehu erupted again yesterday, belching smoke, rocks and lava several kilometres into the sky. Hot lava flows threaten to engulf ski fields, the famous Chateau tourist hotel and the township of Ohakune. Residents and shopkeepers are preparing to evacuate and most, like Mayor Sarah Dogood, agree they have little choice but to leave their homes.

News-maker: There is no way we can risk the safety of our kids and our families by staying put. If we lose everything we may be financially ruined, but at least we'll be alive.

Reporter: Chief vulcanologist Joe Blow says he expects Mount Ruapehu to continue erupting for several days, and he warns of new fissures in the crater lake.

NATURAL SOUND

A reporter covering the Mount Ruapehu eruption recorded reaction to the natural phenomenon in a local pub. But back in the newsroom her actualities missed a vital element. She was sent back to the mountain to get the rumble, hiss and roar of the mountain erupting as background noise. Make sure you capture quality natural sound to edit into stories. Sound effects are important for authenticity and interest in radio news, and add to the dramatic effect of visuals in television news.

TIPS FOR BROADCAST INTERVIEWING

These tips have been compiled after talking with experienced broadcast journalists about the dos and don'ts of broadcast interviews.

1 Listen, listen and listen

The most important advice for anyone conducting a broadcast interview is to actively listen to what the interviewee is saying. Interviewing is primarily a listening exercise. In broadcast interviewing you often only get one chance—particularly if the interview is live.

Top New Zealand radio and television interviewer Dr Brian Edwards believes you need to put aside your prepared interview structure in favour of following a listening lead:

> If somebody hangs a bait in front of you and it's a good piece of bait you've got to take it. If you are not listening you're going to miss it and that will frustrate your listener or viewer. So when somebody says, 'Yes, I did go to university, this was just after I murdered my second wife' and you say 'What subjects did you do at university?', the listeners and viewers know you're not listening. A good interviewer is constantly monitoring what's going on (personal interview with Dr Brian Edwards).

2 Establish rapport

Forming some sort of rapport with the person to be interviewed before the interview is absolutely critical to what happens at the interview. Dr Edwards says:

A lot of young interviewers both in news and current affairs and in the more personality-driven interviews walk in and say, 'Hi, my name is Jeanette and can you come through to the studio?' They will ask the first question in such a way that the interviewee goes in absolutely cold, has no sense of relationship with the interviewer and takes a long time to warm up and may not warm up at all. You must form a rapport, and that involves developing certain intuitive skills (personal interview with Dr Brian Edwards).

3 Avoid 'yes' and 'no' answers

Do not ask the bad broadcast question that results in a 'yes' or 'no' answer such as: 'I understand you saw the mountain erupt?' Questions should be phrased so that the person being interviewed does the talking. For example, 'What did you see when Mount Ruapehu erupted?'

Do ask questions that stimulate conversation and prompt questions that will interest your audience. 'What', 'How' and 'Why' questions are often useful starting points. 'How would you describe . . .' and 'How would you explain the background . . .' are other invitations to news-makers to do the talking.

4 Be kind to amateurs

Some news-makers are 'oncers'. They are in the right place at the wrong time or the wrong place at the right time and witness tragedy, accidents, war, natural disasters or unique events. Amateur news-makers have little knowledge or understanding of the intricacies of broadcast interviews and aren't used to dealing with the media. Good broadcast journalists make a distinction between those who know how to use the media and those who don't. You need to be kinder as an interviewer to those with no experience of the news media. Radio New Zealand's political editor, Al Morrison, says:

> With politicians an interview that has a degree of entrapment, draws them to a point and then whams them with a question out of the blue is legitimate. It isn't as if you are talking to someone who isn't media savvy and who you couldn't expect to be, like someone at an accident site (personal interview with Al Morrison).

At the other end of the scale some public figures are so adept at interviews that you can ask them for a ten-second 'grab' on a particular issue or event, and that's precisely what you'll get.

5 Guide the interview

In a media-centric world victims should, on cue, say that their plight is terrible, victorious sport winners should be ecstatic and gracious about their opposition in equal measure, and those who survive death-defying accidents should talk of miracle escapes. While these reactions are the ones journalists pray for, news sources are not always so obliging. As a reporter you know what you want recorded from the people you interview. So how far can you go?

Most broadcast reporters believe that guiding is appropriate so that those making the news say the right things and provide usable recordings. But it is inappropriate to coach people you interview or to put words into their mouths. Al Morrison agrees:

You often have to repeat questions and sometimes you actually have to stop midstream and do a little training and say, 'Look, I'm not trying to put words into your mouth but what you're saying to me that's interesting is this and this and this ... do you think you could put those three things together in one statement' ... there's an element of training to that which I don't have a problem with because talking into a microphone is not something that people naturally do (personal interview with Al Morrison).

6 Keep on track

News-makers can quickly go down a different track during an interview. You have to keep the interview focused on what it is the public wants to know. Sometimes it is the answer to one question only.

If you ask a question and somebody sort of strolls off and leads you on to asking a couple more questions about another subject which may well be interesting, that's fine, but come back again. Always come back again. Even if it requires making a note in front of yourself saying, 'Ask that question' (Hill 1996).

Kerry O'Brien says he doesn't have particular tricks in the way he does interviews.

I simply endeavour to understand as much as I can by way of background reading on the subject, and try to focus in on its essential elements. What are the things that the public would really want to know about this, which are the most interesting and compelling aspects? What is the time that I have available? How much can I realistically hope to fit into that time? And I then order the questions accordingly (personal interview with Kerry O'Brien).

GETTING THE GRAB: THE HARD NEWS INTERVIEW

The key to getting the grab is timing and the right question. In hard news interviews the questions are likely to be closed questions, questions that are quite specific and intended to restrict the focus of the answer to the question. In an interview about euthanasia on Radio New Zealand, Kim Hill followed up a television story about a tetraplegic who had broken his neck in two places in a truck accident. The tetraplegic could not move his limbs, could not breathe without a ventilator and had written to the health authority requesting the right to end his life. Twelve days had elapsed between the time he was filmed about his euthanasia request and the story's broadcast, during which time the patient felt more positive. Kim Hill wanted to explore the issue of a patient's change of mind about euthanasia with a hospice medical director. After setting the scene Kim asked a series of focused, closed questions in a hard news interview conducted live.

The questions were direct. She asked whether it mattered that television had filmed the patient twelve days before screening the program and in that time the tetraplegic might have undergone a change of mind. She also challenged the interviewee about the logic of patients assessing their lives and deciding that living a poor quality of life was not something they wanted. In the course of the interview she very directly asked the medical director if during the time he had worked at the hospice he had changed his mind about euthanasia. The medical director replied that yes, when he first went into hospice work, 'I was right down the end of the spectrum that said euthanasia is bad and we must not even consider it.' Since then numbers of people had spoken to him about the wretched state of their lives, and he felt more empathy and understanding with them. 'But I think that I still haven't changed,' he said.

During the hard news interview Kim Hill set the scene, introduced her interview guest, asked short closed questions that focused the interviewee, listened to the replies and followed up leads, asked the interviewee the right questions and then asked the tough question that forced the interviewee to reveal his feelings about the purpose of life and euthanasia. While the sensitivity of the subject was acknowledged, the relevant, 'hard' questions were asked and radio listeners felt they had been part of a purposeful conversation. That is the essence of a hard news broadcast interview.

THE SOFT NEWS INTERVIEW

'Oprah's White House special: Winfrey's gift to Obama for Christmas is softball questions' (Kinon and Nagraj 2009).

As the above title suggests, Oprah was not interested in producing a serious, hard-hitting television interview with the Obamas. Journalists Cristina Kinon and Neil Nagraj indicate that although Oprah had been in pursuit of an interview with the First Family since Obama's win in the presidential election, what Oprah was interested in was 'not about grilling the President' but making sure that the interview felt 'comfortable' (Oprah quoted in Kinon and Nagraj 2009).

Perhaps as an explanation for her motive Winfrey says of the special: 'I wanted to be at the White House during Christmastime and to experience their first Christmas at the White House.' She also mentions that the special had 'been in the making for a very, very long time' (Oprah quoted in Kinon and Nagraj 2009).

Oprah's interview questions about the Obamas's Christmas gifts demonstrated a focal point in that she commenced with questions about their childhood memories of their favourite Christmas gifts and followed this with questions about the gifts the Obamas were going to give each other. Notably, the interview questions weren't complicated and were good examples of 'open' questions. Below is an excerpt from the interview that demonstrates these points:

Oprah: Your favorite gift as a child?

President Obama: Well I got a bike one year and I think you know getting that first big-kid, 10-speed bike: That's always special . . . I remember that one. You know, I do remember the one time I met my father, he was visiting during Christmas and he gave me a basketball and—the degree to which I came to love basketball—it wasn't until much later in life that I realized 'Actually, he gave me that basketball.' I think there was some cause and effect there, in terms of the degree to which I just ended up taking up the sport as a kid who didn't know his dad.

Oprah: Do you remember what your favorite Christmas gift was as a child?

First Lady: Oh it was a doll house and it was a metal doll house with plastic furniture but it was and I remember I really didn't know how to set up a house so I had all the furniture lined up along the walls as opposed to nestled around the fireplace, but I loved that little doll house.

Oprah: Well now you get some practice here—goodness gracious. Doll house . . . I asked this question to some of my friends and they all said Easy-Bake Oven. Did you have an Easy-Bake Oven?

First Lady: Oh I did have an Easy-Bake Oven but you know once you run out of the mix it's like you're done with it.
Oprah: (*laughs*) Yeah you're done with that—
President Obama: You couldn't get more mix?
Oprah: It doesn't come with more mix, the Easy-Bake Oven.
President Obama: But can you order more mix?
First Lady: Nowadays it's easy—
Oprah: Probably now you can go online and get more mix—
First Lady: When we were little—what you got—that's what you got. (Excerpt quoted in McAdam 2009: 1–2; original emphasis).

What is interesting about the above interview excerpt are the candid replies provided by the Obamas as well as Barack's unexpected contribution to the Easy-Bake Oven discussion. The discussion could easily be one that has taken place at home during a conversation at Christmas dinner with family and friends. These revelations, however, were broadcast by the American Broadcasting Company (ABC) on Sunday, 13 December 2009. As a public relations exercise it works, and as a personalised insight to the First Family this interview contains all of the elements that make it appealing to a wide audience—humour, childhood reminiscences, and a subject close to everyone's heart (Christmas) as well as an Oprah guided discovery tour of a White House Christmas.

Soft news interviews on radio and television have two things in common. They are extended conversations with people telling stories, and they employ open questions. Dr Brian Edwards says the extended broadcast interview probably has only one question: 'Tell me about it, tell me your story . . . in a nutshell you are looking for stories. Stories, stories, stories. Examples, illustrations, people want to hear stories . . . that's what makes an extended interview work' (personal interview with Dr Brian Edwards).

As the master of thousands of soft broadcast news interviews, Dr Edwards offers the following tips.

Chase away butterflies

Helping interviewees overcome nerves is essential so that they perform well. You must recognise how nervous many people are at being interviewed for radio and television even if the interview is an extended, soft interview and even if they are experienced.

If what you're looking for is a successful newsy conversation in which both parties are at ease, then maybe a bit of flattery up at the front of the interview does not do any harm. Most of my intros to people I was interviewing on radio on Saturday morning were actually very flattering. You looked across the table and you could see the interviewee melt a little and lose some of their nervousness because they think, 'This fellow had a bit of a reputation as a hard-liner', but this isn't going to be like that.

As well as flattery, try reassurance and self-disclosure along the lines of, 'Look, I'm sure you're feeling a bit nervous, I'm getting a bit nervous myself.' Relaxed interviewees will be more candid, reveal more of themselves and enjoy the interview experience.

Don't irritate the interviewee before the start

A common failing of inexperienced interviewers is that they irritate or annoy the interviewee before the interview has started. Displays of indifference and discourtesy to the newsmaker in the studio can be off-putting. Chatting to someone in a civilised and interested manner before the interview is a way of establishing mutual respect even if hard questions have to be asked later.

> You don't realise it, but people expect a degree of respect and may feel that they've put themselves out a bit to be there and do the interview. They don't want to be treated like a disposable piece of meat. Once you get into interview mode you may have to turn the knife a little, but don't go out and be hostile before you start.

Think about the opening question

An extended interview has a rhythm of its own, and listeners and viewers need to feel that the interview went somewhere. Interview structure is important so that the conversation has a satisfying form to it. A soft interview needs an introduction, development of the material and a conclusion of some sort, with some light and heavier exchanges in between. The opening question sets the scene.

> I'm a great admirer of actor John Hurt and was looking forward to doing an interview with him. I met him for about five or six minutes just before the interview, and he looked really hung over. In addition to being really hung over he was chain smoking. As an interviewer you will often pick up on little, seemingly inconsequential things as an entrée to the interview. They may be little things you have noticed or things someone has told you. An interviewee will be chatting to you while a record is playing, and they'll mention a reminiscence of something about themselves. That's often a very valuable way of forming early rapport. So we chatted for a moment or two about his smoking, and then when I started the interview I began by asking him

about his smoking, in a totally disapproving way. 'Why are you smoking cigarettes? . . . Don't you know it's bad for you?' It rocked the interview and took me twenty minutes to get back on track, so that was really bad judgement.

Watch your time

There is a danger of loss of control in the soft news interview, and as the interviewer you have to exercise time judgement. Ask yourself, 'How much time can I afford to spend on this subject?' If you spend too much time on a tangential subject you risk missing the core topic that might be further down the track.

Dr Brian Edwards. (Photo courtesy of Dr Edwards)

Open questions can be hazardous. There is a risk that the interviewee will wander off down some track, so you're always a ringmaster in an interview and you're always controlling it, keeping it on track and bringing people back to the point. I did an appalling interview with the wife of a great pioneer film-maker in which I spent a whole lot of time talking to her about her background and almost never got around to the movie-making. That was a terrible mistake.

Keep eye contact

During the interview it pays to keep up a non-verbal dialogue with the interviewee, which helps them relax, be spontaneous and enter into the spirit of the conversation.

Eye contact with your interviewee is terribly important. You never take your eyes off the person. You treat them like a lover so they lose all sense of everything around them. Women say they find men who pay them attention attractive. It is the same with interviews. You pay the interviewee a lot of attention.

Involve the interviewee in the dynamics of the interview

Novice interviewers often bury their heads in their notes the whole time. Interviewers do have to refer to written material or question sheets during an extended interview to refresh themselves about a line of questioning. But involve your interviewee in the interview process. Tell them about the studio and the procedures.

I will often say to an interviewee that I'll be looking down a bit because I've got my questions on my sheet but please don't think that I am not interested in what you're saying. Tell them what the game is all about.

Be wary of clippings

Research is essential for extended interviews. Often soft interviews are conducted with personalities and celebrities, visiting stars and sports people who have been written about comprehensively. These clippings form part of the celebrity archaeology that all broadcast interviewers undertake in the research process. But be wary.

A danger of clippings, of course, is that they may not be accurate. You could find yourself saying to a studio guest, 'You did this and that' and the person responding, 'No, I bloody did not' and 'Who told you that?' and then you're in trouble. Cuttings that come from the tabloid press or women's magazines can be dangerous. On the other hand, something you found in the *Women's Weekly* twenty years ago might make a brilliant line of questioning.

Try for a good end

Just as an interview needs a good opening to grab listener and viewer attention so it also needs a good end to be memorable. You want to try to finish well, and it is important in long interviews to have an end in mind. Former New Zealand Prime Minister Sir Robert Muldoon would note the wind-up cues in live television studio interviews and turn abruptly to the camera and commandeer the last seconds with a direct message to his own advantage. As an interviewer you need to be in control of the interview and ensure that you, rather than your guest, end the interview. Beware, too, the interview that dribbles to an end. You will have lost the audience.

HORROR BROADCAST INTERVIEWS

All broadcasters can remember interviews they'd prefer to forget. Sometimes the interview is a disaster because the equipment fails, you forget to turn on the microphone, the batteries in the recording device fail or the vision is unusable for technical reasons. In these cases the interview might not get to air. In other cases horror interviews occur not for technical reasons but because you get off on the wrong foot with an interviewee, you ask a question the interviewee objects to or you persist with a line of questioning that doesn't work. Because you're on-air or in a studio with live audiences these can be nerve-racking experiences for the interviewer, the news-maker and the audience. Dr Brian

Edwards recalls a disaster of an interview with American jazz great Duke Ellington.

> I had a question that had come up in the research and was along the lines of: 'There seems to be no evidence of you having done anything to really support the struggle of black people in the United States.' He was immediately infuriated by the question and turned to me at the interview and said, 'This interviewing business isn't your bag.' Afterwards I realised that his contribution to the black movement of the United States was his music and not standing up and making speeches. It was a really misjudged question and it was not meant to be that sort of interview (personal interview with Dr Brian Edwards).

Don't become the story

An interview between *Newsweek* journalist Sarah Lacy and Facebook CEO Mark Zuckerberg was not only seen to be disappointing but unfortunately was one where the inteviewer was moreso focused on herself instead of the interviewee or for the benefit of the live audience who attended the South by Southwest interactive (SXSWi) media event. South by Southwest (SXSW, Inc.) is a privately owned company located at Austin, Texas, that organises conferences for the interactive media industry.)

Daniel Terdiman of CNET News and author of the story 'Journalist becomes the story at Mark Zuckerberg SXSWi keynote' admits he felt at odds writing this particular story as it is essentially a review of another journalist's performance. However, as justification for his criticisms, there were a number of examples he could provide that proved his point, including constant interruptions and speaking over Zuckerberg (Terdiman 2008: 1, 3).

A further departure from a professional interview occurred when an audience member demanded that Lacy 'Talk about something interesting!' (Terdiman 2008: 2). The remainder of the audience responded with an almighty cheer. Lacy in turn responds, saying, 'Try doing what I do for a living . . . It's not that easy' (quoted in Terdiman 2008: 3). Terdiman noted that 'the crowd was not sympathetic, and some demanded that she turn the microphone over to the audience so they could ask questions' (Terdiman 2008: 3).

Some of the tweets that were sent during the interview weren't particularly complimentary. Robert Scoble, a well-known video blogger, posted this tweet: '[The] audience in the back of the room is totally ripping her apart. Saying she should just ask questions, not put herself in the interview' (quoted in Terdiman 2008: 3).

However, Terdiman also acknowledges that her questions were solid and some of them caused Zuckerberg to become uncomfortable. This was revealed when 'he kept asking her how she had learned about certain points she was asking him about' (Terdiman 2008: 4).

In Terdiman's opinion, however, the result was an interview that saw Lacy 'injecting herself into the story in a way that was far out of balance with the dynamic that should have been in evidence during a discussion between her and the CEO of one of the most talked-about companies in the world' (Terdiman 2008: 3). It was her style that Terdiman questioned the most as it alienated the audience from the outset—'she seemed flirty with him, trying to put on an air of being his buddy, when what the audience wanted was to listen to Zuckerberg talk' (Terdiman 2008: 4).

Lacy did try to apologise to Zuckerberg, saying, 'I'm sorry to torture you for an hour'; however, this was not received very well (Terdiman 2008: 5). Throughout this interview, not only was the interviewee treated disrespectfully, but it wasn't until approximately 10 minutes prior to the end of the interview that Lacy allowed audience participation in a Q & A session—the audience of 2000 was not at all happy about this. The interview was one hour in length (Terdiman 2008: 1, 4).

Freezing and 'umms' and 'ahhs'

As well as technical troubles and bad judgement calls by the broadcaster, interviews can be fraught when either the news-maker or the reporter freezes. Radio New Zealand's political editor Al Morrison says the really horrific broadcast interviews are the ones in which people freeze into silence. He recalls a radio station crossing to a reporter for a live account of a parliamentary protest demonstration. The reporter froze and couldn't speak. Back in the studio the silence had to be filled with improvised talk while other linkages were made. When amateur news-makers who are not accustomed to being in the news freeze in front of the microphones or cameras, it is often because of the unnatural intrusion of the technical equipment. They suddenly realise that the world is watching and listening to them, and they become nervous. It pays to try to minimise technological intrusion in certain sorts of broadcast interviews.

'Umming' and 'ahhing', mumbling and poor enunciation and pronunciation turn off the audience in broadcast interviews. They are very obvious when reporters are doing pieces to camera. Breathing exercises before facing the camera and going on air, thinking about the question and not your answer, slowing your speech down and consciously trying to avoid 'umms' are all techniques used by broadcast journalists to avoid the verbal fumbles. Al Morrison says he's very aware of his voice as a radio broadcaster. While he walks into work he does voice exercises, stretching his vocal chords, talking to himself out loud and thinking about the art of performance as a broadcast journalist.

VIDEOJOURNALISM

Some journalists in smaller television stations today have added pressures resulting from modern technology and staff cuts. These 'videojournalists' have to not only conduct their own interviews but also get video footage of the interview and sometimes even edit the piece. Videojournalists need to be flexible and multiskilled to gather and produce quality stories. Armed with a digital camera and tripod, these video-journalists must ensure that they obtain good footage and sound as well as strong 'grabs'. There are several advantages of being a 'one-person team'. An Australian newspaper article entitled 'Low-cost quality' notes: 'Video-journalism has come of age when reporters on a program of the stature of *Dateline* (SBS) are heralded at Australian journalism's premier awards night for work they reported, produced, directed, filmed, and at least partly edited' (Plane 2000: 14). *Dateline* journalist Mark Davis describes it as a 'humanistic approach to news' whereby the reporter has to 'think about the people rather than the story'. 'It's more intimate,' he says. 'People will invite one person to stay, or ride in their car, which they wouldn't do with a three- or four-person crew' (Davis quoted in Plane 2000). There's also a huge cost advantage, not just in crew costs or cheaper cameras but also in things like travelling on a bus rather than a hire car. 'It's a real advantage with this stuff that people are off your back about cost,' says Davis (Davis quoted in Plane 2000).

REFERENCES

Australian Broadcasting Corporation (ABC) TV 7 July 2008, Helen Thomas, 'Elders—Part 4', *Enough Rope*, interview transcript, pp. 1–13, http://www.abc.net.au/tv/enough-rope/transcripts/s2296751.htm, accessed 3 March 2010

Hill, K. 1996, *Advanced Interviewing Skills for Journalists*, National Diploma in Journalism, Wellington Polytechnic and the Open Polytechnic of New Zealand, quoted with permission from the broadcaster

James-Enger, K. 2009, 'The cost-conscious freelancer', *The Writer*, vol. 122, issue 5, pp. 36-7, http://www.writermag. com; Australian/New Zealand Reference Centre database, Accession no. 37365141, pp. 1-2, accessed 15 March 2010

Kinon, C. and Nagraj, N. 11 December 2009, 'Oprah's White House special: Winfrey's gift to Obama for Christmas is softball questions', NYDailyNews.com, http://www. nydailynews.com/, accessed 8 January 2010

McAdam, T. 13 December 2009, 'We'll be skipping Oprah and the Obamas on TV tonight', *Examiner.com*, pp. 1-4, http:// www.examiner.com/, accessed 18 January 2010

Paul, I. 14 January 2010, 'Tech tools tell the story of earthquake in Haiti', *PCWorld*, pp. 1-5, http://www.pcworld.idg.com. au/article/332380/, accessed 21 January 2010

Plane, T. 14-20 December 2000, 'Low-cost quality', *The Australian*, Media, p. 14

Simons, M. 2007, *The Content Makers: Understanding the media in Australia*, Penguin Books, Camberwell, Vic

Terdiman, D. 9 March 2008, 'Journalist becomes the story at Mark Zuckerberg SXSWi keynote', *Geek Gestalt*, CNET, pp. 1-6, http://news.cnet.com/8301-13772_3-9889528-52.html, accessed 26 February 2010

The Podcast Network 2007, 'About the Podcast Network', http://www.thepodcastnetwork.com/about, accessed 1 February 2010

8

TELEPHONE AND EMAIL INTERVIEWS

One newspaper editor was known to call cadets into his office, pull the phone out of the wall connection and throw it across the room to show his displeasure at its overuse. A bit dramatic perhaps, but it certainly got the point across!

While the face-to-face interview is the ideal way of gathering information from primary sources, it is steadily becoming a less common method used by journalists. Today more interviews are being conducted by fewer staff who are turning to faster methods of news gathering. The two most common time-saving methods used today are telephone and email interviews. While they do not have the advantage of providing non-verbal cues (such as eye contact and body language), they are very convenient for both the interviewer and interviewee. This is particularly the case with email interviews where those involved in the exchange are in different time zones. As Australian journalism educator and author Barbara Alysen says,

'A reporter who doesn't have to leave the office is a reporter who can squeeze more stories into a working day.' However, she agrees that the 'downside is that the interviewer can't use the normal methods of establishing rapport such as eye contact and body language' (Alysen 2000: 131).

Newspaper editors tend to frown on the use (or overuse) of the telephone interview whereas broadcast news editors generally accept it as a necessity imposed by tight deadlines. The former believe journalists should be out and about talking to people and looking for stories on a continual basis—not waiting for the phone to ring, or using the phone to contact people for local rounds. While a high percentage of face-to-face interviews may be possible for print journalists, radio journalists producing five news bulletins or more each day have little choice but to rely heavily on the phone to interview sources and record sound bites.

Most journalists go to great lengths to avoid the telephone interview—preferring the face-to-face exchange. However, telephone interviews do provide some important clues, including tone of voice, silence, volume and laughter. It is essential, too, that the journalist gives encouragement to the interviewee when conducting an interview on the telephone.

One cadet who always spent extra time talking to police sergeants, ambulance officers and other daily contacts was often rewarded with front-page stories. She tells the tale of chatting away about a local football match one day when the police sergeant interrupted with: 'You haven't heard, have you?'

'About?' she asked.

'Go down to the wharf right now, and there'll be a story for you,' he replied.

The story was a double murder, and an exclusive page-1 scoop for the reporter.

BEWARE OF THE AVOIDANCE FACTOR

While email and telephone interviews are convenient for reporters, they can be equally convenient for elusive news sources. Politicians, sports stars, public officials and celebrities sometimes don't want to reply to email inquiries. Some also have gatekeepers fobbing off phone calls. There is also a raft of telephone paging devices and mobile phones that incorporate technology allowing the receiver to know who is calling before answering. This permits avoidance behaviour. Reliance on email or telephone interviewing is probably a mistake if the news source wants to play hard to get. Only persistent and ingenious methods of making contact with elusive news sources works.

Both telephone and email interviews have a certain protocol, and steps that should be taken to increase the success of the exchange. Twelve essential steps for conducting telephone and email interviews, with explanations and advice for each step, are provided below. However, in any exchange, whether face to face or via a telephone or computer terminal, politeness and curiosity are still essentials.

THE TELEPHONE INTERVIEW

1 The first step for any telephone interview should be to introduce your organisation, yourself and the fact that you want to do an interview for publication—print or broadcast. Put your name second, as people sometimes miss the first few words of a phone conversation. You should quickly follow this introduction by asking the interviewee if they have a few minutes to spare. If they don't, respect this, and ask when you might be able to call again to interview them. If they do indicate they have the time, repeat the details about the interview, what information you would like from them and where and when it might be used. If you can avoid it, try not to pressure people into giving you detailed

information in a hurry. This may not always be possible, particularly for radio journalists, but most people will not appreciate being given a tight deadline and may either refuse to be interviewed or be abrupt in their responses.

2 Thank anyone who takes the trouble to return your messages—it doesn't happen that often!

3 As a general rule smile while you are talking on the phone. Try it, and you will realise that it makes you sound much more encouraging and friendly. However, you may not want to do this in every telephone interview, particularly if you are asking 'tough' questions. Don't talk too loudly or softly; just use your ordinary speaking voice. If you're using a mobile phone, make sure you're in an area where the signal is strong and won't drop out.

4 Restrict your icebreaker. As a general rule you are using the telephone as a time-saver, so get to the interview as quickly as you can.

5 Have your questions or keywords well organised before you get on the line. You don't want to be wasting the other person's time while you are searching through pieces of paper to find your list.

6 Keep your questions simple. This should always be the case, but it is particularly difficult for interviewees to remember long and complex questions on the telephone. Two sentences is the maximum—one sentence is better. Don't be afraid to ask for examples, and even description. The latter is particularly important if you are conducting a feature interview over the phone. Journalism educator and author Carole Rich writes about an American reporter, Nancy Tracy, who had a way of 'almost seeing through the telephone':

> She would ask her sources for details. She asked what they were wearing, what they were doing, what they

were thinking, how they were coping and reacting. An introduction from a feature story she wrote includes this detail obtained on the phone. 'Some days when the pain isn't too bad, he stands by the front door, watching trucks roll by on Highway 41 on their way to Macon. Then the memories come flooding back, the crash, the pain' (Rich 2000: 132).

7 Take down your notes as quickly as possible. If you're recording the interview for broadcast or for your own record, you must tell the interviewee before you start.

8 Ensure you understand all the answers given. If you don't, ask again or request a simpler explanation. Don't be afraid to admit you don't understand—you can't be an expert in every field.

9 Listen carefully and be ready to follow up any unexpected answers.

10 Be polite from beginning to end. Keep your cool—even when your interviewee does not.

11 Obtain the correct spelling of the interviewee's name and their correct title. Repeat these over the line if you are unsure.

12 Don't forget to obtain contact details. Try not to call people outside work hours—unless unavoidable. Thank the interviewee for their valuable time.

THE EMAIL INTERVIEW

The email interview is an excellent way to contact your sources for information, and far cheaper than using the telephone. Contacting people quickly and cheaply anywhere on the globe is the major advantage, though your emails can easily be ignored. These interviews can either be conducted in 'real time', with both the interviewer and interviewee logged on at the same time, or can be sent and delivered as ordinary emails with the interviewee replying in their own time.

Author Jane Dorner says, 'Email interviewing doesn't replace intuitively following your subject's lead and getting clues from tone of voice, but telephone interviewing was itself always a poor second to the face-to-face chat' (Dorner 2000: 32). Rich agrees, noting that, 'Although it is not preferable to interviewing by telephone or in person, email is an option for interviewing sources who can't be reached otherwise or can't spare time for other forms of contact' (Rich 2000: 102–3). Andrea Carson, former industrial reporter with Melbourne's *Age*, says she used email more for establishing and maintaining contacts rather than for interviews. She believes there's no pressure on the recipient to answer the questions, and in her role as industrial reporter the questions were often tough ones that require this pressure. Andrea says she was more likely to use email for introducing herself to new and potential contacts and, after she established the contact, for maintaining communication.

Reporter Richard Trow uses email interviewing in his job as defence reporter for *The Dominion* and as a former reporter for the New Zealand paper's 'Infotech Weekly' section.

I started to use email interviews, particularly for offshore interviews, and to overcome time differences around the world. I found that they were very useful for background interviews and for conducting friendly interviews and engaging people in factual debate. I very quickly came to the conclusion, though, that there were difficulties with email interviews if you wanted to ask tough questions (personal interview with Richard Trow).

Richard says the reporter gives away too much power to the news source in these email interviews. 'If someone doesn't want to answer, or claims not to be there, you have lost control.' Richard says email interviewing also allows a news source to take material and show it to public relations people before replying. He has two tips for email interviewing:

1 Structure your questions in point form, one by one. If you lump what you want to know together then news sources can leave out difficult questions, or ignore questions. Following this advice you would conduct your email interview as: (a) How was the fraud discovered? and (b)Why did you leave the company? And so on.
2 Avoid unduly irritating a news source by activating the urgency of your email interview. Richard says it irritates him when he receives 'High urgency' and 'Top priority' emails when they are not, so he recommends you don't use this protocol.

> And *DO* be careful about assuming the veracity of a news source in an email interview. Someone else could be logged on or sitting at the computer other than the source you think you have quoted accurately. While an email response may be an insurance against misreporting claims because you have a verbatim record, it may be no defence if it wasn't written and sent by the source you thought you were in email conversation with (personal interview with Richard Trow).

The following are recommended steps for an email interview.

1 The first step is an introductory one. For the email interview there really is a protocol for organising an interview because you can't determine immediately if the interviewee has time to be involved in an interview. So send an email to your interviewee introducing yourself and your

organisation and requesting the interview. Do not include anything more than an introduction here. Jane Dorner, author of *The Internet: A Writer's Guide*, believes: 'Online interviewing is exactly like traditional interviewing. The first email should be exploratory, introducing yourself and your publication. Use the same formality register as you would in any other circumstance; email doesn't give you a licence to be casual' (Dorner 2000: 33).

2 The next step should be to ensure that the interviewee is well aware of the purpose of the interview. Rich notes that you should also clarify your purpose very early and 'make it clear that you intend to use the email message in a news story. Personal email messages are not intended for publication' (Rich 2000: 134).

3 If they agree to an interview, decide how it is to be conducted—in real time or in the interviewee's own time. Real time's probably preferable as you can get the information you need immediately, follow up on any answers you don't understand and ask for clarification and more information as required. It also means the answers are more spontaneous.

4 If you have chosen a real-time interview you should start with some sort of summary statement on what you hope to achieve in the interview, and determine how long the interviewee has to 'talk' to you.

5 Ask your first question. Because the questions are available visually (on screen), they can contain far more information than questions asked on the telephone or during a face-to-face interview. Jane Dorner believes that 'using email to interview forces you to be more prepared by formulating questions in advance. It's less intrusive, allowing you to ask your questions at any hour of the day without bothering anyone' (Dorner 2000: 32). However, she cautions that it's best to start with just a few questions. 'A whole barrage of questions in one email is off-putting and will make the

subject feel they are writing the article for you. It's best to bounce to and fro and build up an iterative picture' (Dorner 2000: 33). The more questions you include, the more you reduce your chance of getting a response.

6 Don't be afraid to ask for clarification, or perhaps an answer worded in a simpler way.

7 Be prepared to follow up unexpected answers, but don't allow the interview to stray too far from the original topic.

8 Determine how long you are prepared to wait for an answer. If you haven't heard from the interviewee after a couple of minutes (allowing time for formulating and typing an answer and then sending it), you may want to send a short note asking if they need the question reworded or clarified.

9 Make sure you have your questions or keywords in front of you, and check these to make sure you have covered them all before concluding the interview.

10 Check the spelling of the interviewee's name and their correct title. Often an abbreviated version is used in emails, and sometimes a nickname is used. Always confirm these details.

11 Ensure you have contact times, numbers and addresses before signing off.

12 Thank the interviewee for their valuable time. Print out the full exchange immediately, and don't forget to contact them again when the article comes out.

One of the major advantages of an email interview is that you have a written record of the questions and answers—so you can't be accused of misquoting. The major disadvantage, particularly with an exchange conducted over a period of time (not 'real time'), is that the answers are not spontaneous and may lack 'colour'. As Jane Dorner points out, the 'email interview gives your subject time to think, so chances are that they will express what they really want to say more carefully. You can always email back an amended version of the quote if need be and get a quick "agreed" in return' (Dorner 2000: 32).

As email interviews are in written form, you must ensure that your questions are well framed and not vague. You are also relying heavily on the fact that your interviewee will be 'good talent'. However, be prepared for the fact that you may be interviewing someone who is not conversant with email, has difficulty formulating written answers (though they may be extremely articulate on the phone or in person), and who may use streams of bureaucratic jargon. Your interviewee might also be a 'two-finger typist', so responses could be a long time coming.

Email interviews have also been broadcast during television programs, when the source was hesitant to appear in person. Visually, what the audience sees projected on a computer screen is the equivalent of the email interview.

ELECTRONIC DEVICES FOR INTERVIEWING

Interviewers now also have further choices at their disposal in relation to digital devices that can not only record interviews but also assist in delivering them. The communication devices journalists now choose to carry can include a BlackBerry, Apple iPhone or just an average mobile phone, all of which can offer email and multimedia messaging options, the functionality of a camera to take photos, with video capabilities and web browsing. The emergence of social media such as Facebook, Twitter and YouTube that can be accessed via the mobile phone has virtually reinvented the interview and the way it can be conducted in relation to its immediacy. The downfall of immediacy is that the interview is also vulnerable to bias, misinterpretation and inaccuracies.

An alternative to pen and paper is the Smartpen—which records sound, as well as your notes—which can also be saved to your PC.

TIP

Ensure that the battery of your mobile is fully charged or can be charged at some juncture and, better still, carry a spare battery. An additional memory card is also worth considering.

REFERENCES

Alysen, B. 2000, *The Electronic Reporter*, Deakin University Press, Geelong, Vic

Dorner, J. 2000, *The Internet: A Writer's Guide*, A & C Black, London

Rich, C. 2000, *Writing and Reporting News: A Coaching Method*, 3rd edn, Wadsworth, Belmont, CA

9

USING THE INFORMATION

'Well, we knocked the bastard off!' Sir Edmund Hillary on conquering Mount Everest, 1953 (Knowles 1998: 149).

'That's one small step for man, one giant leap for mankind' (Neil Armstrong as he walked on the moon, quoted in Knowles 1998: 13).

Quotes are the pearls of journalism. We recall brilliant lines by great and ordinary people that have been quoted by journalists. Some quotes are immortalised and become part of our shared culture and history. Lines from former Australian political leaders, such as Sir Joh Bjelke-Petersen's 'feeding the chooks' (referring to speaking to the media) and Don Chipp's 'keep the bastards honest' (when talking of other political parties), are still frequently used today. Quotes—when to use them and when to avoid them, when to paraphrase and when to use direct speech—are only a few of the judgements that reporters have to make quickly after they have conducted an interview.

Quotes can:

- bring a living, active feel to a story
- lend authenticity
- allow audiences to hear the voices of people in the news
- provide an accurate summary
- provide proof of what was said in controversial issues or legal contexts
- catch provisos, nuances and distinctions in passages of speech
- provide colour, tone and flavour to a story
- make the story contemporary with the use of colloquialisms.

DO USE direct quotes from an interview when the news source says something better than you can as the reporter. When we were interviewing for the first edition of this book, veteran New Zealand broadcaster Dr Brian Edwards spoke of how he maintains eye contact with his interviewees. 'You never take your eyes off the person. You treat them like a lover so they lose all sense of everything around them' (personal interview with Dr Brian Edwards). A great quote like that should never be paraphrased. Imagine how it would sound or read if you took the words out of direct speech.

DON'T TRY to use direct quotes when the news source is simply reciting factual information or giving you omnibus information. Avoid padding out a story with quotes or simply repeating material with quotes.

TIP

Before rushing to the computer or telephone to use the information you've gathered in the interview, pause for a minute to:

- mark the best quotes
- read over all that was said for context, flavour and tone
- work out who else needs to be interviewed for a story and
- identify the angle.

HOW TO GET GOOD QUOTES

Some sources are living, breathing quote machines. Everything they say is rich in tone and flavour. Others, such as politicians, can be guaranteed to drop at least one great line per news conference. Sometimes the best quotes come as brilliant flashes from unlikely people. In other cases good quotes are hard to come by. The news source is wary, wooden or monosyllabic. In these cases you have to work hard in an interview to get good quotes. Here's some tips for extracting the best possible quotes from those you interview:

- Try to relax the news source.
- Establish trust between yourself and the source by using good interpersonal skills and displaying empathy.
- Spend extra time in person with the news source or on the phone—it might yield dividends.
- Actively listen for clues in answers that will lead to a question that flushes out a choice quote.
- Ask quality questions that are more likely to produce quality responses.
- Try the occasional spontaneous but intelligent 'left field' question in soft news interviews.

You should immediately recognise a good quote when it is uttered. Either during the interview or immediately afterwards, mark or underline the good quotes so that you can angle your story around the best quotes. Use the top quotes from the interview as direct quotes. Paraphrase the factual information or the pedestrian parts of the interview.

'I WAS MISQUOTED ...'

This is the most common complaint to editors and regulatory bodies about reporters. Misquotation is easy to do and painful to rectify. There are different types of complaints about misquotation that you should recognise. The following types of complaints are typical:

- complaints from people who are accurately quoted but don't like the reaction to the words quoted
- complaints from news sources who didn't know they were being quoted
- complaints from people who were caught off-guard and are now embarrassed
- complaints from people who are genuinely misquoted, and
- complaints from people who think they should have been quoted and weren't.

Misquotation can occur directly because the words as printed were not a direct quotation, or indirectly because the context in which the quotes are published distorts the meaning. Kerry O'Brien says he doesn't believe in the practice of changing the order of answers or changing the actual questions used, as this can 'alter the nuance' and give an unrealistic view of the context in which the statements were made (personal interview with Kerry O'Brien).

There is no single rule about what to do when a news source complains about misquotation. If you have recorded the interview, you will have evidence about the accuracy of the quotation. Similarly, shorthand notes provide a measure of protection. When the complaint is vexatious you should expect support from the newsroom or the publisher of the story.

In cases where you've made a mistake, it pays to put it right as soon as possible.

ARE QUOTES SACRED?

This was the heading in an *American Journalism Review* article discussing whether journalists should ever change quotes. There are usually newsroom rules about whether or not quotes are to be changed. Should someone's comment be made grammatically correct, embellished so that it is more colourful or altered so that it is easier to follow? There has always been wide disagreement over the extent to which quotes should be altered. Often, too, it is not the reporter who alters the quote but the next person in the news production chain.

There has never been a perfect news source, one that didn't ramble, one that didn't interpolate with the odd 'umm' and 'ahh', one that didn't speak in half sentences. For example, what do you do about the news source whose subjects never agree with their verbs? If there were a perfect news source, then there would never be the temptation to clean up quotes (Germer 1995).

While there are no fixed rules, the following points of guidance about altering quotes from interviews are useful:

* You may wish to fix grammatical errors and correct syntax, and delete 'umming' and 'ahhing'.
* In most circumstances it is better to paraphrase than make someone look stupid because they have been quoted literally. However, there are times when it is appropriate to quote even if the news source will suffer embarrassment.
* Never change quotes so that the meaning conveyed is different from that intended by the news source.

- It can be dangerous to add material to quotes.
- It can be dangerous to delete material from quotes.
- Watch slang and abbreviated language.
- Ensure that you are alert to racist, sexist and defamatory quotes from news sources. It will be no defence to say you quoted the source accurately!

> Many journalists new to the profession believe that because a defamatory statement has been quoted, they are not liable. This is not true. Both the journalist and their organisation can be sued for defamation as the publishers of the statement.

BEWARE MIXING AND MATCHING QUOTES

A trap for reporters is to take quotes from previously published or broadcast material and add them to current stories. Extra caution is needed if your feature story on a controversial doctor contains six paragraphs of quotes, two taken from an interview given five years ago, two quotes taken from yesterday's recorded interview and two quotes taken from last week's telephone interview, put together as a seamless flow as if the source was speaking yesterday. This type of quote collage can lead to distortion.

For example, the Australian Press Council upheld a complaint by the National Front of Australia against a Sunday newspaper that quoted the Front's chairman saying, 'We have been well trained in the use of guns and explosives if we have to defend ourselves against political opponents.' The Press Council established that the quoted remarks were a composite of remarks allegedly made by the chairman at various places and various times.

The paper was clearly at fault in presenting remarks as a direct quotation when this was not the case. The Press Council said readers were entitled to believe that direct quotes were what they purported to be, and it censured the paper (Australian Press Council 1979).

MAKING IT UP

One thing that you should never do is to fabricate quotes. The New Zealand Press Council censored *New Truth* over a complaint by the Prostitutes' Collective following an article in which the paper attributed a quote to a particular woman. In her complaint the woman said she had not been interviewed and the words were not hers, and they were not the words of anyone else from her organisation. The editor said a freelance reporter had produced the story and had assured the paper that the comments attributed to the woman were accurate but had come from another member of the collective who asked, as a matter of protocol, that they be attributed to the woman as coordinator. The Press Council said the newspaper had attributed a quote to the woman but it now acknowledged that it was not hers.

'At best this can be seen as a foolhardy lapse likely to cause distress to the individual involved and threaten the reputation of newspapers generally. The attribution of quotes which had not been made can be regarded only as disreputable journalism and reprehensible in the extreme' (New Zealand Press Council 1999: 26).

Stockwell and Scott, authors of the *All-Media Guide to Fair and Cross-Cultural Reporting*, believe it's important that when 'people are claiming some authority to speak on behalf of others, [the journalist should] be sure that such authority has some basis in reality' and 'be sure to determine when someone is speaking as an individual and when that person is speaking on behalf of a group or organization' (Stockwell and Scott 2000: 19).

SWEARING—EXPLETIVE DELETED OR EXPLETIVE REPORTED?

What happens in an interview when a public figure lets down their guard and swears? Should you report profanity, obscenity or swearing? Should you protect public figures from themselves when they swear? There are no set answers to these questions. Whether to delete or report expletives depends on:

- what sort of publication or broadcaster you work for
- the context in which the swearing occurs
- who says it
- commonly accepted standards of decency and good taste, and
- whether the expletive adds something essential to the story.

What is acceptable for one publisher or broadcaster may be unacceptable for another. Even within daily journalism there is often a division of opinion over whether to report swearing.

Some guidance to commonly accepted standards of decency and good taste comes from the information produced by bodies such as the Australian Communications and Media Authority and the New Zealand Broadcasting Standards Authority, which monitor trends in public taste and regularly publish lists of the acceptability and unacceptablility of bad language in broadcasting (Dickinson, Hill & Zwaga 2000).

JUDGEMENT CALLS

Other judgements reporters must make in using interview material involve whether the information given to you was 'on the record' or 'off the record', and how to check the accuracy of what was said. You need to be aware that different stories call for different judgements and that different media have specific rules or practices that may not be universal. For example, some newsrooms do not allow you to use anonymous sources unless the journalist is experienced and there is confidence in the source. In broadcasting, however, paraphrasing someone's comments so the audience doesn't know the source of the news is common.

You should also keep in mind that some issues such as the use of anonymous sources and whether stories should be checked with interviewees are subject to a good deal of healthy and critical debate in journalism generally. For example, the O.J. Simpson case generated so many stories based on anonymous sources that Los Angeles *Daily News* writer Ray Richmond satirically suggested setting up a 'Rent-a-Source' service for reporters (Shepard 1994).

ANONYMOUS SOURCES

The use of anonymous sources is a hot topic in journalism. There are those who insist that the use of named sources is critical to the purpose and credibility of journalism. They argue that not naming sources devalues the news and leads to lower journalistic standards. Public trust in news reporting is damaged if people can't see and hear who is being quoted. Some journalists believe that using unnamed sources leads to lazy journalism and allows politicians and public officials to take 'cheap shots' against opponents under the veil of anonymity.

Defenders of anonymous sources, on the other hand, including Watergate reporter Bob Woodward, believe that some important stories would never surface without them. Woodward says unnamed sources can be a valuable tool. 'The job of a journalist, particularly someone who's spent time dealing in sensitive areas, is to find out what really happened' (Shepard 1994). He says there is no way of reporting on the inside of agencies like the CIA, Pentagon or the White House without using anonymous sources, because people won't necessarily go on the record. The Australian Press Council says that 'the quoting of anonymous sources is common and justifiable practice in political reporting' (Australian Press Council 1979).

TIPS

Here are some useful tips on naming sources:

1 Treasure the value of named sources that give your stories credibility.
2 Use confidential sources only for very important information.
3 Always verify information from confidential sources with another source.
4 Don't allow sources to go 'off the record' unless there are exceptional circumstances.
5 Know what 'off the record' means. It does not mean you can't use the information if you can get it elsewhere, but it does mean you can't attribute the information to the news source who has given it to you on an 'off the record' basis.
6 Never betray a confidential source. However, you may have to disclose the identity of unnamed sources on a confidential basis to your superior.
7 You must always question the motives of unnamed sources.
8 Be particularly cautious about unnamed sources who express opinions about others or who are judgemental.
9 Readers, listeners and viewers should be told why a source's identity is not being disclosed.
10 Beware the anonymous source who is available only on the telephone and can't be traced—never trust information from anonymous sources you've never met.

Never bow to pressure to name confidential sources. The Australian Press Council says, 'It is a principle well established in journalism, and one which the Press Council habitually upholds, that sources of information published in newspapers are not to be inquired into' (Australian Press Council 1978). Journalists are staunch defenders of the principle of non-disclosure in controversial cases and have been prepared to risk prison in contempt of court cases.

HONOURING THE DEAL

Some stories involve reporters agreeing to the terms under which the interview will be conducted and how the material will be published or broadcast. Very often this is a confusing area for members of the public who have little experience of the news media. It can also be difficult for reporters. The deals you make on the spot to get the story may, in fact, contradict your newsroom policy or the protocols of the broadcaster or publication you are working for. A process of negotiation then begins.

Most reporters abide by the convention that once they have established their identity and the organisation they work for on the telephone or face-to-face with a news source or inter-viewee, then anything the interviewee says from that point can legitimately be reported. Many news organisations have a 'no deals' policy and believe that proper sourcing and attribution establishes the credibility of news.

SHOW AND TELL?

An unwritten taboo in journalism is showing or reading back a story before publication to a news source. Showing what you've written can allow the source an opportunity to meddle with your story. Sources might want to alter the tone or emphasis as a consequence. Readbacks also take time and threaten deadlines. Again there is a wide division of opinion in journalism about the practice. On the one hand, it has been called a 'moronic practice' that relegates reporters to glorified secretaries. On the other hand, at the *Missourian*, the paper run by the University of Missouri School of Journalism in Columbia, readbacks are standard practice and called the 'accuracy check' (Donald W. Meyers quoted in Shepard 1996).

It is best to follow local rules about showing a story to a news source after the interview and before publication. While readbacks are not normally done, there may be some exceptional circumstances in which you choose to show back quotes. These include:

* reassuring yourself that you got it right
* reassuring a source who is innocent of the media's ways
* ensuring that complex, technical subjects in science, technology or business are correctly reported, and
* building trust with an important but reluctant source.

Another technique might be to read back the interviewee's quotes before you leave the interview. This protects you in terms of accuracy but does not damage journalistic integrity.

THE USE OF RECORDED TELEPHONE CONVERSATIONS

Some reporters record all telephone conversations as an insurance policy. They follow the practice whether or not the person at the other end is aware of the recording. Under section 123 of the *Broadcasting Services Act* 1992, industry groups have developed codes of practice in consultation with the Australian Communications and Media Authority. Once implemented, the ACMA monitors these codes and deals with unresolved complaints made under them (www.acma.gov.au).

The Commercial Television Industry Code of Practice (within the ACMA's register of codes of practice) notes that for Interviews and Telephone Conversations (section 1.25) first and foremost: 'Licensees are subject to relevant Federal and State law when broadcasting interviews and telephone conversations' (Commercial Television Industry Code of Practice January 2010 p.5 in www.acma.gov.au). Further to this, confidential information is still governed by common law in order to 'protect privacy and restrict the obtaining and publication of information' (Commercial Television Industry Advisory notes January 2010 p.65 in Commercial Television Industry Code of Practice at www.acma.gov.au).

The media must tread a fine line between ensuring material used for broadcast doesn't invade an individual's right to privacy, while at the same time deciding if there is justifiable reason for broadcast in the public interest. The Commercial Television Industry Code of Practice (Clause 4.3.5) addresses the requirement of an individual's privacy, which they state should be observed with the exception that 'there is an identifiable public interest reason for the material to be broadcast' (Commercial Television Industry Advisory Notes January 2010 p.63).

Additional guidance on the use of confidential information is provided by the ACMA's *Privacy Guidelines for Broadcasters*, and note that before broadcasting, consideration should be given to whether the public interest is 'served by disclosure of the material' (Commercial Television Industry Advisory Notes in the Commercial Television Industry Code of Practice January 2010 p.63 in www.acma.gov.au).

An ACMA investigation in 2009 followed a complaint concerning a story 'Hunting the Tigers', which was broadcast on the SBS program *Dateline* on 15 March 2009. The complainant alleged that among other concerns: 'the reporter recorded the telephone conversation with the Defence Department military liaison officer, for purposes of broadcast, without the latter's knowledge' (ACMA Investigation Report—*Dateline* broadcast by SBS TV on 15/3/09 p.4 in www.acma.gov.au).

The Relevant SBS code 1.8: Interviews, Talkback and Audience Responses states that:

> SBS will not transmit the words of an identifiable person unless: that person has been informed in advance that the words may be transmitted; [and] in the rare case of a recording obtained without permission or an interview for which consent has been withdrawn, the broadcast is demonstrably in the public interest.

> SBS submitted that the broadcast of the material was 'demonstrably in the public interest' as it showed the extent to which media access to those people injured or left homeless by the fighting in the north of Sri Lanka was being restricted at that time.

The ACMA Finding was that 'SBS did not breach clause 1.8 of the code'. (ACMA Investigation Report—*Dateline* broadcast by SBS TV on 15/3/09 p.4 in www.acma.gov.au).

For legal and ethical reasons, journalists in Australia should always tell someone when they want to record them over the phone.

REFERENCES

Australian Communications and Media Authority (ACMA), '2010 Commercial Television Industry Code of Practice', http://www.acma.gov.au/, accessed 16 September 2010

——2 December 2009, 'AMCA Investigation Report—*Dateline*', http://www.acma.gov.au, accessed 16 September 2010

Australian Press Council 1978, Adjudication No. 39, October 1978 APC 16, http://www. austlii.edu.au/au/other/apc/1978/16.html, accessed 10 March 2010

—— 1979, Adjudication No. 55, May 1979 APC 8, <http://www.austlii.edu.au/au/other/apc/1979/8.html>, accessed 10 March 2010

Dickinson, G., Hill, M. and Zwaga, Z. 2000, *Monitoring Community Attitudes in Changing Mediascapes*, Broadcasting Standards Authority, Wellington, NZ

Germer, F. 1995, 'Are quotes sacred?', *American Journalism Review*, September, pp. 34–7

Knowles, E. (ed.) 1998, *The Oxford Dictionary of 20th Century Quotations*, Oxford University Press, New York, USA

New Zealand Press Council 1999, *The Twenty-seventh Report of the New Zealand Press Council*, New Zealand Press Council, Wellington, NZ

Shepard, A.C. 1994, 'Anonymous sources', *American Journalism Review*, December, pp. 20–5

—— 1996, 'Show and print', *American Journalism Review*, March, pp. 40–4

Stockwell, S. and Scott, P. 2000, *All-Media Guide To Fair and Cross-Cultural Reporting*, Australian Key Centre for Cultural and Media Policy, Nathan, Qld

10 KEEPING SAFE

The news-gathering interview involves journalists in situations with legal and ethical consequences. As a reporter it is important to develop intuitive antennae that will alert you to legal and ethical concerns when interviewing. But you are not on your own. Remember that different media organisations make judgements about ethical dilemmas and legal risks all the time, and you can ask for advice from colleagues and news superiors. In this chapter we use a drugs scenario as the background to explore issues about media law and reporters' ethics to help you think about some of the interview contexts involved.

SCENARIO

A police reporter, Jane Light, notices from reading the obituary columns an unusual number of death notices for young teenagers in the same month. She makes inquiries of a friendly police source and finds that the deaths are heroin overdoses and that all the teenagers are from the same school.

The source also tells her that one of the dead youngsters is related to a prominent television personality, and there are rumours that the TV star introduced the teenagers to cannabis before they graduated to heroin. Her police contact reluctantly tells her in confidence that a major heroin cartel is operating between Australia and New Zealand and that the deaths are related to one shipment. Jane asks her police contact if she can talk to her editor in confidence about the information. Her editor agrees that she can work on the story in her own time, but tells her to report back to the newsroom with any developments.

As Jane makes more inquiries she finds a lot of little pieces emerging. In interviews with relatives of the dead teenagers, the TV personality's name is mentioned several times. One parent said the TV star was always present at parties attended by his son. 'I suspect he introduced my boy to hard drugs,' he said. A women's magazine featured a cover story with the TV star distraught at the graveside of the man's dead son. There are also rumours of police corruption. Several prominent business people are alleged to be laundering drug money.

Privacy

Jane decides to start her investigation by interviewing friends and family of the young teenagers who've died of drug overdoses. There is wide public interest in preventing heroin abuse in the community, and Jane believes that her readers need to know what's happening. She realises that this is a sensitive time to call grieving family and friends. She will rehearse her opening before telephoning or visiting the families, but is aware that she might be rebuffed. When she calls she will pay her condolences and ask gently but persuasively for an interview. Jane believes that the publicity given to interviews with the families might act as a deterrent and that she might pick up information for her wider investigation into the drug cartel.

How many times can a reporter telephone and request an interview?

First, Jane will have to take into account the general ethical presumption that grieving families should be treated with dignity, compassion and respect. The Australian Journalists Code of Ethics, developed by the Media, Entertainment and Arts Alliance (MEAA), states in Code No. 11 that journalists should 'Respect private grief and personal privacy. Journalists have the right to resist compulsion to intrude' (MEAA 1999). Similar guidance is provided by the United Kingdom's National Union of Journalist's (NUJ) Code of Conduct, principle No. 6, 'A Journalist: "Does nothing to intrude into anybody's private life, grief or distress unless justified by overriding consideration of the public interest" (NUJ 1936-) and that of the US's Society of Professional Journalists (SPJ), Code of Ethics, under the heading of 'Minimize Harm', 'Journalists should be sensitive when seeking or using interviews or photographs of those affected by tragedy or grief' (SPJ 1996-).

Second, Jane should know that merely telephoning someone once or twice or visiting their home seeking legitimate information will not constitute a nuisance. However, harassment by persistent telephone calls or badgering relatives unnecessarily is another story. In an unusual New Zealand case, a newspaper publisher was found guilty of misusing a telephone by making annoying calls to victims of a rafting tragedy on the pretext of a journalistic inquiry (Burrows and Cheer 1999). Even though he'd been given a clear message not to call back after the first call, he made three calls to one victim. In the Australian context, Pearson states that 'continuous telephone calls, persisting despite requests that they cease, could be considered a nuisance, while a series of phone calls merely seeking an interview for a story would not normally be considered as such' (Pearson 1997: 226).

Despite her motive for seeking a compelling story that might prevent further drug deaths, Jane needs to be aware that she is still intruding at a time of grief and that it is rare for anyone who has just lost a loved one to welcome the attention. She had heard rumours of one television journalist who had turned up at the home of one of the families and could not understand why his offer of a box of iced doughnuts was not accepted as entrée into the grieving parents' home. Jane knows that the hardest interviews reporters have to undertake involve death and grief. Some reporters are better at these interviews than others, but even experienced journalists find them tough.

Deathknocks

Deathknocks, as they are called (see Chapter 1), involve telephoning or approaching grieving family members or friends about a person who has died immediately after the death. There is no easy way to undertake deathknocks. Such interviews require courage and sensitivity. Reporters face a range of reactions in asking to speak with families at times of grief. Some people are adamantly opposed to any intrusion whatsoever and are angry at the approach. Others welcome the reporter as someone to talk to, for the opportunity to publicise something they feel is wrong and to acknowledge a loved one.

Jane knows from media coverage of the Port Arthur massacre in Tasmania in 1996, when thirty-five people were shot dead, that ordinary people can be thrust into the media limelight despite their right to 'private grief'. She has been reading *To Have and to Hold* (1997), Walter Mikac's book co-written with Lindsay Simpson, detailing the tragic loss of his wife and two daughters who were shot and killed in the massacre. A friend of Walter's wife, Lindsay was working for the *Sydney Morning Herald* at the time and had been sent to cover the massacre. Reluctantly she contacted the Mikac home, where the phone was answered by the family doctor. When she explained that the call was part of her work for the

Herald and not a personal call, the doctor replied by asking whether she thought that Walter had the right to grieve in private. She agreed that he did, and ended the call (Mikac and Simpson 1997).

But as Jane knows, not all the media dealt with the case so ethically or responsibly. The media attention was immediate for Walter and the other victims. On trying to enter the Port Arthur historic site the day after the massacre, Walter saw a 'huge contingent of vehicles, police milling around and people standing behind an impromptu barricade'. He said:

> The media line acted like a starting line rather than a barricade. Bodies with microphones and cameras surged towards our vehicle. I didn't want to be photographed like this, but then again I wanted the world to see the tears that were welling up in every cell of my body. I could hear the shutters flickering. At that moment I knew that I was no longer just a husband and father mourning the loss of his life's essence—whether I liked it or not, I had become one of the living casualties, the walking wounded from Port Arthur. The image of my distressed, slumped body trying to deny the inevitable would be splashed all over the newspapers the following day (Mikac and Simpson 1997: 5–6).

Jane is aware that some organisations today are advocating different approaches to deathknocks—one, to use an intermediary to talk to the media (such as a counsellor), and another, to have just one journalist conduct the interview, which can then be disseminated to the rest of the media. In a case where a three-year-old girl was abducted and killed by a fourteen-year-old boy early in 2001, the local chaplain represented the family in dealings with the media. In Mikac's case, he said:

I also had to tackle the strange experience of being a celebrity—for which I had no training and no time to prepare. The media wanted a piece of the action now. I was newsworthy and deadlines could not wait ... But on the Tuesday after the shooting, I decided I would speak to Ray Martin on *A Current Affair*. If the media train was approaching, I was going to meet it head on. I could dictate the terms. I would speak once and that was it (Mikac and Simpson 1997: 135).

Jane knows that quotes from family members are highly newsworthy when young people have tragically died of drug abuse, so how does she reconcile the wider public interest with the right of personal privacy?

She refers to the New Zealand Victims' Task Force *Victims of Crime, A Training Kit for Journalists* (1993) for general principles. These and other pointers are included here.

1   Use a neutral third party like a police officer, family friend or funeral director to make the first approach.
2   It is legitimate to ask whether there is someone in the family who would like to pay tribute to the dead person.
3   Persuasion but not compulsion is the tactic that secures the best result.
4   If the family declines an interview, that should be the end of the approach, although the reporter could leave a card or a contact number should the family change its mind.
5   If during an interview a family member becomes upset or wishes to exit, the reporter should acknowledge the rights of the interviewee.
6   Ensure that during the interview the reporter does not reveal sensitive or upsetting information that may have been concealed from the family by the police or other authorities.
7   Request photos of the dead person only at the end of the

interview and after you have built an empathetic relationship with the interviewee.

8   Funerals are not generally the best times for the first
    approach because they are highly charged with emotion
    and grief.

9   Be aware that the interviewee is grieving and may regret
    the revelations when they are published or broadcast. Not
    all family members will welcome the publicity.

The Victims' Task Force training kit was produced after thirteen
people died in a tragic slaying by gunman David Gray, at the
tiny South Island hamlet of Aramoana, New Zealand, in 1990.

The Dart Center for Journalism and Trauma at the University of Washington produced another booklet, *Tragedies
and Journalists: A Guide for More Effective Coverage* (written
by Joe Hight and Frank Smyth), which begins with a chapter
on interviewing and tips for interviewing victims. The first tip
emphasises the need to 'Always treat victims with dignity and
respect—the way you want to be treated in a similar situation.
Journalists will always seek to approach survivors, but they
should do it with sensitivity, including knowing when and how
to back off' (Hight and Smyth 2004: 7).

Off the record

After two unsuccessful attempts to speak to the parents of some
of the dead youngsters, Jane hears that the father who told her
about the TV star is willing to talk to her again—but only if
some of the information is 'off the record'. After speaking to
her editor, who agrees to the conditions, the interview is set up
at his house.

While Jane is conducting the interview she notices some
family photographs (as does the photographer who is with
her). While the father is out of the room answering the phone
the photographer urges Jane to take one of the photos, but she

refuses. She asks the father some personal questions, but when he declines to answer them she does not persist.

As promised, the story the next day is about the drugs issue, but the headline has been sensationalised compared to the story written by Jane. It reads: 'Heroin death destroys local family', which in no way reflects the content of the story. She complains to the editor, and decides to call the father to apologise. Unfortunately he decides he will no longer deal with Jane because of the story's treatment.

Investigative journalism

Jane is troubled by the sensationalism. She has learned that journalism involves tensions between newsroom decisions and her own personal feelings about building trust with people she interviews. She decides to keep on digging and interviewing others to get the drugs story. She is inspired by examples of journalistic tenacity. Prize-winning Kiwi investigative journalist Warren Berryman defines investigative journalism as 'an attitude of mind towards a story so that you never leave something that begs the question why ... the investigative journalist will keep on niggling away' (quoted in Booth 1992: 162). Investigative journalist Chris Masters, of ABC's *Four Corners*, describes investigative journalism as a 'big dig'. He says despite the considerable resources of the media, the big dig happens all too infrequently. A big dig can improve public perceptions about an important issue virtually overnight. He adds, however, that a big dig can take up to three months to complete at some pain to colleagues and bosses (Masters 1992: 15–16).

During the first interview Jane receives some possible leads regarding the heroin deaths, so she requests time to do some more research. The newsroom is quite large and fully staffed (with no one away on leave) so the editor reluctantly agrees to give her a few days. Jane is pleased to have even this small amount of time. She decides to do another library search first, and talk to the senior police reporter, before heading out.

Anonymous sources and contempt of court

Jane goes back to the original source of information (the obituaries) and also looks through file copies of local papers, including her own. She finds several stories on drug raids conducted by police, with the names of two officers appearing frequently in these stories. Jane decides that these names are her next lead, though she is unsure how much help will be provided regarding her investigations.

Both officers refuse to talk to Jane when she phones and suggest that she contact the police media liaison officer. She does, but again runs into a brick wall. Several days later, however, she is contacted by her friendly police source, who has heard talk around the station that she is still investigating the heroin deaths. They agree to meet in a small suburban coffee shop on the opposite side of the city to the police station. Her source asks for complete anonymity. The MEAA Code of Ethics points out that 'where a source seeks anonymity, do not agree without first considering the source's motives and any alternative attributable sources. Where confidences are accepted, respect them in all circumstances' (MEAA 1999). Broadcasters too are obliged to monitor the integrity of their sources. The UK's National Union of Journalist's Code of Conduct and that of the US Society of Professional Journalists Code of Ethics advocate similar approaches.

Jane agrees to his request and decides to meet him, but tells her editor where she is going and the time she thinks the interview will take. Jane knows that if this case ever goes before the courts, she could be charged with contempt of court (perhaps even gaoled) for withholding the name of the source, but she is willing to do this to get the story. However, if she breaks the trust it would damage not only her reputation but also that of investigative journalists generally. On talking to the police officer Jane learns that a small number of police are involved in covering for heroin traders, some connected to local businessmen. Her friendly police source is alarmed at police corruption but does not want to betray his colleagues. Jane believes he is genuine and that she has a 'big story'.

Jane now has to independently corroborate the source's information so that she can honour her promises of anonymity and confidentiality to her friendly policeman. He had given her two names of people he was sure would help—one a fellow 'honest cop' who also wanted to remain anonymous, the other a relative of one of the dead teenagers. She knows this will be a good start, and will hopefully lead to other sources to confirm the police officer's story. At this point the relative is the only person willing to go on the record.

What if they won't answer?

Jane goes back to her editor and tells him what she has found. She requests more time. He too can sense it is a big story and grants her another week. Jane knows she will have to put in a lot of overtime even with this extension. She is also concerned with what could happen if no one will answer her questions, and she comes away from these two interviews empty-handed.

As a relatively new reporter, Jane needs to develop her own style. Here is how an experienced journalist like Chris Masters describes his approach.

There are few worse setbacks than an exclusive witness's firm refusal to talk. I have, in my time, sweated over many a telephone. There is no technique that guarantees success . . . All I can say is it helps to be honest. When a journalist calls, people's bullshit detectors are instantly turned on. It is also worth remembering there is no long-term profit in deceiving a witness. If you do end up in court, you want them as friends, not enemies. I find it also helps to be curious.

Everybody has a story to tell and there is a frequent compulsion to tell it. Some of the best 'investigative' journalists are, quite simply, good listeners (Masters 1992: 48–9).

Establishing credibility and chequebook journalism

Jane is not concerned about the validity of information from the honest cop, but is concerned about the information she might receive from the relative of someone who died of drug abuse. When she first contacts the relative, he asks how much the newspaper will be paying for the story.

The controversial issue of chequebook journalism currently bedevils the news media. It is a common practice in women's magazines, tabloid journalism and commercial television, but seldom occurs on community newspapers, such as Jane's, nor on Radio New Zealand, the ABC or SBS. Chris Masters says:

> Chequebook journalism is a common, unattractive feature of the profession. If you pay a witness for a story the evidence is immediately devalued, certainly in the eyes of the courts. The theory is that witnesses who work for reward might be encouraged to say anything. Even worse, they might be persuaded by a larger sum to later reverse their story (Masters 1992: 58).

Jane persuades the relative that he could be discredited in the community if it became known that he had profited from the tragedy.

Reputation and defamation

Jane decides to follow up on the parents' claims about the TV star who apparently introduced their children to heroin. Journalists need to be cautious about some issues when interviewing to avoid defamation. The first tip for Jane is to know something about what defamation is. This allows her to identify potential defamation when she is conducting interviews. Reporters are not expected to be experts and there is no single definition of defamation, which makes it a difficult area. Remember, however, that ignorance of defamation is no protection. Jane should at least know that defamation is about:

- injuring someone's reputation by publishing or broadcasting a false statement, and/or
- lowering the opinion of the person in the eyes of ordinary people, and/or
- bringing the person into hatred, ridicule or contempt, and/or
- saying something about someone that tends to make others shun or avoid them.

If Jane uses the father's quote 'I suspect he introduced my son to hard drugs', would the quote be defamatory? First, for the TV star to sue for defamation he would have to prove that the publication referred to him. Australian magnate Kerry Packer successfully sued for defamation despite being referred to only as 'Goanna'. Obviously if the TV star was named that would be identification. In this case he wasn't named. But the TV star could claim that the published statement refers to a small group of people—local TV stars—of whom he is a representative. How many TV stars are enough? As Pearson states, 'The courts have decided to view such cases in terms of the size of the class being defamed, the generality of the charges made and the extravagance of the accusation, with each case according to its circumstances. The test is whether ordinary, reasonable individuals would believe the defamatory statements referred to the plaintiffs' (Pearson 1997: 108). Burrows and Cheer note that 'a statement that "all the lawyers in the town of X are incompetent sharks", there being only four lawyers in that town, would ground a defamation action by each of the four' (Burrows and Cheer 1999: 38).

So what if Jane quotes the father as making the statement? Is she safe? No. Jane does not have a defence simply because she is quoting someone else's words. Nor does it matter if Jane didn't intend to defame the TV star, she is still liable. It will not help the reporter, either, that she was merely reporting a suspicion or a rumour. The reporter has to prove the rumour was true, not just that there were rumours around about the TV star and drugs.

So how can Jane report the TV star's alleged involvement? Can she put the rumours to him and report his response? Burrows and Cheer warn against such a strategy: 'A defamatory rumour coupled with a denial of a rumour might still leave the matter capable of a defamatory meaning' (Burrows and Cheer 1999: 27). It is dangerous to use the device: 'TV star X today denied rumours that he introduced teenagers to hard drugs following the deaths of several youths from overdoses', because some ordinary readers, listeners or viewers may suspect that he did.

The best way for Jane to defend herself against a defamation action is to prove that the TV star introduced teenagers to hard drugs. Remember that, if it comes to court, the TV star does not have to prove he didn't; the reporter has to prove he did. Truth as a defence is based on the notion that a person's reputation is based on actions and behaviour and that publication of the truth merely broadcasts the reputation to a wider audience (Pearson 1997). If the journalist does have proof then there is clear public interest in exposing a public figure who is involved in the distribution of drugs.

Jane has conducted dozens of interviews in her investigation and feels frustrated that she cannot write her big story. She spends several hours with the relative and publishes a specific story about his knowledge of the parties where teenagers were using drugs. After the story is published a school friend of the dead boy telephones Jane and tells her that the TV star had also offered him heroin at a party. He says he is prepared to tell his parents and have a story written so that no other friends die.

Jane tells her editor, who contacts the paper's lawyer. The lawyer suggests that Jane interview the boy with his parents present and show them her copy before publication (an exception to the paper's policy).

Jane has a scoop—a story that is both of public interest and in the public interest. She has succeeded through luck, persistence, building trust and effective interviewing.

Remember that more experienced journalists such as your chief reporter, editor or news manager have first-hand experience of tricky interview situations. Always keep them informed and take early advice about legal and ethical matters. It can save painful apologies, damaged journalistic reputations and expensive payouts. Keep them informed of all your dealings with interviewees that may have ethical or legal ramifications. Many organisations also have legal advisers and trainers who can provide guidance and help to check work if you are unsure.

REFERENCES

Booth, P. 1992, 'Investigative journalism: The New Zealand experience', in *Whose News?*, (eds) M. Comrie and J. McGregor, pp. 161–9, Dunmore Press, North Palmerston, NZ

Burrows, J. and Cheer, U. 1999, *Media Law in New Zealand*, 4th edn, Oxford University Press, Auckland, NZ

Hight J. and Smyth, F. 2004, *Tragedies and Journalists: A Guide for More Effective Coverage*, Dart Center for Journalism & Trauma, University of Washington, http://dartcenter.org/files/en_tnj_O.pdf, accessed 15 March 2010

Masters, C. 1992, *Inside Story*, Angus & Robertson, Sydney, NSW

Media, Entertainment and Arts Alliance (MEAA) 1999, *Australian Journalists Association Code of Ethics*, MEAA, Sydney, http://www.alliance.org.au, accessed 3 March 2010

Mikac, W. and Simpson, L. 1997, *To Have and to Hold: A Modern-Day Love Story Cut Short*, Macmillan, Sydney

National Union of Journalists (NUJ) 1936–, *National Union of Journalists: Code of Conduct*, http://www.nuj.org.uk, accessed 26 February 2010

Pearson, M. 1997, *The Journalist's Guide to Media Law*, Allen & Unwin, Sydney, NSW

Society of Professional Journalists (SPJ) 1996–, *Society of Professional Journalists: Code of Ethics*, Eugene S. Pulliam National Journalism Center, Indianapolis, IN, http://www.spj.org/ethicscode.asp, accessed 26 February 2010

Victims' Task Force 1993, *Victims of Crime, A Training Kit for Journalists*, Wellington, NZ

RESOURCES

AUSTRALIA

Access to the Information and Services of the Australian, State, Territory and Local Governments http://www.gov.au/
While it has a long and unwieldy title, this site provides very easy access to government information from around Australia, with links to agencies, departments and specific personnel with contact details.

Australian Bureau of Statistics (ABS) http://www.abs.gov.au
Australia's official statistical service offers publications, spreadsheets and detailed information on areas, including the economy, environment and energy, health, industry and population growth. Expert survey advice and consultancy services that customise data to meet client needs are also provided.

Australian Council for Educational Research (ACER) http://www.acer.edu.au/resources/journalist.html
A resource- and service-based organisation for journalists investigating and writing about educational topics, ACER's website provides expert commentary, media releases and research

reports—a considerable number of which can be downloaded for free.

Australian Government (entry point)
http://www.australia.gov.au/
This site provides easy links to approximately 900 Australian government websites, useful and accessible background information on Australia's systems of government and services in addition to specific state and territory resources. Topics include Australian facts and figures, employment and workplace, immigration, tourism and travel.

Australian News.Net http://www.australiannews.net
This site is particularly useful for the headline news section and includes stories from news wires, worldwide TV networks, prominent newspapers and Australian News.Net journalists. Links to local Australian news sources—for example, key Australian newspapers—are also provided in addition to rural news, finance and sport. A regional map and polls of general interest also feature on this site.

Government On-Line Directory http://www.directory.gov.au/
This official guide to the Australian Government focuses on the organisations, key staff and its structure. There are four categories of information which are representative of the four main components of government. These are:

1 Government Departments and Agencies (within portfolio groupings)
2 Commonwealth Parliament
3 Governor-General
4 Courts and Judges

Contact details for the various organisations and officials are available, as well as functional descriptions. The quick links on the home page also provide access to state and territory government directories.

Journoz.Com http://www.journoz.com/
Designed for journalists and media students, this website supplies access to Internet sources and relevant information via the 'Ethical Journalist's Source Directory' for the practice of ethical Australian journalism. The Journoz organisation is a committed advocate of professional and ethical Australian journalism.

The Melbourne Press Club
http://www.pressclubonline.com/
The Melbourne Press Club's home page includes a link titled 'Resources' which directs you to a variety of helpful and authoritative websites with global coverage pertaining to journalism associations, journalism education and tools—the latter of which includes the highly regarded Newslink website http://www.newslink.org/res.html. This covers industry-related aspects such as editing, reporting and convergence as well as offering search tools, publishing aids, academic resources and a starting point for journalists.

UNITED KINGDOM

British Journalism Review (BJR) http://www.bjr.org.uk
Published quarterly by Sage Publications, London, full-text archived articles are available through a search field. The articles concentrate on analytical-based content and ongoing assessment of the media. The BJR's target audience consists of journalists working in print, broadcast or online forms of journalism, as well as academics and students.

Journalism UK http://www.journalismuk.co.uk
This website is designed mostly to cater for print journalists who either write for UK magazines or live in the UK, and for those

involved in broadcasting and research. News sources, local and national newspapers, film, television and radio organisations and media-related organisations can be accessed as well.

Journalism.co.uk http://www.journalism.co.uk/
Described by this site as 'the essential site for journalists', the Journalism Links Directory provides access to research tools, sub-editing, news agencies and general sites for journalists. The training section includes links to short courses run by Journalism.co.uk, as well as university courses and training news.

The JOURNOLIST http://www.johnmorrish.com/journolist
Produced by John Morrish for journalists, this site has an excellent list of bookmarks available that include search engines, directories and guides, newspapers, reference tools, useful UK tools and sites and Internet search and journalism links.

UNITED STATES OF AMERICA

American Journalism Review (AJR) http://www.ajr.org/
The American Journalism Review website is not only a source of articles about journalism, it also has a wide selection of resources with links to the AJR *Study Guide*, reporting tools, writing aids and journalism organisations. Additional links to news sources include newspapers, television networks, radio, news wire services and media companies.

American Society of Journalists and Authors (ASJA) http://www.asja.org/
This organisation's primary aim is to foster the professional development of freelance (nonfiction) writers. Professional advice is supplied in the form of information sheets, with a resources section providing links to news sites, investigative writers and other writers' organisations.

Associations on the Net http://www.ipl.org/div/aon

The Internet Public Library: Associations on the Net (AON) provides access to professional and trade associations as well as research institutions. This site is divided into easily accessed subject areas such as business and economics, education, science and technology as well as providing links to regional and country information and reference tools. The Internet Public Library is a public service organisation created for the Internet community.

CyberJournalist.net http://www.cyberjournalist.net/

Both a news and resource site, this site's content concentrates on the effect that digital technologies, convergence and the Internet are having on the media. Cyberjournalist.net provides helpful information for journalists producing online and digital journalism, as well as citizen journalists and those report-ing their stories via the Internet. The tips and tools category also provides links to 'New Media Resources', 'News site podcasts', 'A Bloggers' Code of Ethics', 'Legal issues' and 'RSS for journalists'.

Forbes.com People Tracker

http://www.forbes.com/cms/template/peopletracker/index.jhtml

This website enables you to track more than 120,000 executives and those celebrities or wealthy persons that are listed with Forbes, and also provides research information about execu-tives and public companies. Access to current news covering people or companies specific to your tracker includes articles available from Forbes.com and Forbes magazines. Best of all, subscription and email alerts are free.

International Centre for Journalists (ICFJ)

http://www.icfj.org/

The promotion of journalism standards on a global basis is the main focus for this organisation. This is supported by a comprehensive program of digital training that includes practical hands-on training, seminars and workshops. For new and experienced journalists, there are a variety of training manuals to assist with increasing or refreshing skills. Subjects covered in the training manuals include reporting, working with sources and new media, and case studies; information and tools are provided for all skill levels.

Journalism.org: The PEW Research Center's Project for Excellence in Journalism http://www.journalism.org/
This site offers journalism resources with links to tools, ethics codes and publications. The selection of tools is designed to assist journalists working in print, radio and broadcast, online, international and citizen journalism fields, as well as journalism educators, students and newsroom managers. There is an emphasis on news reporting and its analysis, which is supported by empirical research methods. The aim, as indicated by this site's authors, is to promote a better understanding of print journalism based on comprehensive analysis.

LIST OF PERSONAL AND EMAIL INTERVIEWS

Carson, Andrea   October 2000
Davis, Peter   June 2000
Edwards, Dr Brian   October 2000
Faine, Jon   June 2000
Hamilton, John   November 2000
Harvey, Beth   16 February 2010
Hill, Sharon   November 2000
Lyneham, Paul   April 1996
Morrison, Al   August 2000
Munro O'Brien, Jodie   14 January 2010
O'Brien, Kerry   November 2000
Spalding, Sally   July 2001
Trow, Richard   November 2000
Urban, Andrew   April 2000

INDEX

Aboriginal people 62

access 67–9

accidents 137

accuracy 35, 167, 171, 175

actualities 132–4

Alysen, Barbara 3, 11–12, 153–4

amateurs 136–7

ambushes 5

anecdotes 120, 122–3

angles 39, 109–10, 113

annoy 143–4

anonymity 172, 187–8

answers 133, 136, 160–2

appointments 67

Asian communities 77

atmosphere 15, 73, 78

audience 14, 86, 89, 95, 97, 172

Australian Communications and
    Media Authority (ACMA) 175–6:
    Commercial Television Industry
    Code of Practice 176: *Dateline*
    (SBS) 176–7

avoidance 12, 155

background information 24, 32, 34,
    48, 70, 77: knowledge 37–8

Barber, Lynn 61–2, 63–4

Berryman,Warren 186

Biagi, Shirley 89, 112

body language 6, 15, 17, 19, 115, 153,
    154

breathing exercises 150

broadcast interviews 125–51 *passim*;
    intensity 129; intimacy 129

Broadcasting Services Act 1992, 175

Broadcasting Standards Authority
    (BSA) 171

Carson, Andrea 109, 158

catch phrases 65

celebrities 12, 35, 109, 119

CEOs 12

challenge 10, 94, 96, 111, 116

chequebook journalism 189

children 11, 13

choices 92, 94

clarification 93–4

clippings books 40

closed questions 87–8, 94, 139

code of ethics 181, 187

Cokley, John 47–8

computer files 40

computer-assisted reporting 45–6:
    research 48

concentration 16

confidence 34, 65

consequence 87

contact book 57

contempt of court 174, 187

control 64, 105–6, 145, 147, 159:
    interview subject 64

convergence culture 47–8

conversations 62; soft news interviews
    142; telephone 175–6

corruption 9, 109; police 188

courtesy 68, 74

credibility 33: establishing 189; named
    sources 172–3; online content 48;

criminals 13

cultural concerns 62, 76–7

curiosity 17–18, 37–8, 155

daily rounds 7

Dart Center for Journalism and
    Trauma 7, 185

Davis, Mark 151; *Dateline* (SBS) 151

Davis, Peter 13–4, 74

deals 174

deathknocks 5, 7, 182–5

defamation 169, 189–91

Denton, Andrew 125–7

devil's advocate 96–7, 103

Diana, Princess of Wales 2, 4

Dingo, Ernie 32–3, 41, 42

disasters 9, 45, 136

doorstop interviews 4, 5

Dorner, Jane 158, 160–2

dress 66

Edwards, Dr Brian 135–6, 142–8, 165

electronic devices 162; Apple iPhone
    36, 130, 162; BlackBerry 36, 130, 162

electronic filing 40–1

email interviews 18, 153, 155, 157–62

emotion 3

enunciation: mumbling 150

equipment 81, 111, 113

ethics 179–92 *passim*

evasion 12

events 7–9, 14

exclusive 8, 66

experts 11, 13–14, 37, 49

eye contact 15, 59, 145–6

fabrication 170

Facebook 45–6, 148

face-to-face interviews 19, 154

fact-fudging 34

Faine, Jon 10, 16, 19

feature story 44, 109, 117–24 *passim*

first impressions 73

flash drives 59

focus 61, 65, 85, 105–6, 139

freelance 13, 46, 130

freezing 150

gatekeepers 68–9, 155; persistence 68;
    surprise tactics 68

general knowledge 74, 78

general rounds 8

genres 9

Google 50: Google Earth 36, 51, 67

Gosper, Kevan 10

grabs 2, 132, 151

Granato, Len 117, 120–1

Grimshaw, Tracy 6

Grundy, Bruce 50, 77

guiding 137–8

Hamilton, John 77, 80–1

handshakes 75
Hansard 49
hard news 109–17 *passim*, 139–40
Harvey, Beth 83–4
Hill, Kim 35, 139–40
Hill, Sharon 5–6
human interest 109, 117
hunches 39
hypothetical questions 96, 103

icebreaker questions 73–82 *passim*,
    111, 113, 120, 156
immediacy 4, 129, 162
information: background 33–4,
    biographies 77; finding 49;
    gathering 153; rankings 92, 94
innocents 12
Internet searches 50
interviews: accessing 67–9; adversarial
    9; ambushes 5; arrive early 111,
    113; background 14; broadcast
    125–51; challenging 12, 108;
    deathknocks 5–7, 182–3; definition
    3; doorstop 5; electronic 4;
    electronic devices 162; email 4,
    18, 153, 155, 157–62; emotional
    3; equipment 113, 120; event
    8, 67; face-to-face 19, 153; fact
    and opinion 3; feature 3, 81; first
    impressions 73; group 8; guiding
    137; hard news 3, 109–17· *passim*,
    139–40; human interest 3, 109, 117;
    interest 61; news 111–7 *passim*,
    139–40; online 160; point of 61;
    print 108–24 *passim*; psyching up
    56–7; 'real time' 18; relevance 61;
    requesting 160; rounds 7–8; satellite 4,

18–9; Skype 4, 18–9, 133; soft
    news 3, 109, 117–24 *passim*, 140–7;
    sound bites 2, 154; styles 9–11;
    techniques 14–18; telephone 4,
    153–7; terms 174; time and place
    for 111, 112; time judgement 145;
    timely 61; vox pops 4
investigative journalism 51–2, 109, 186
irritation 143–4
issues story 34

James-Enger, Kelly 130–1
Jenkins, Henry 47–8
journalists: broadcast 11, 125–51
    passim; chequebook 189; electronic
    4, 5; humble 37; investigative 49,
    187, 189; magazine 3; print 5;
    professional 77; resources 49; skills
    11, 74; styles 9–11; television 5;
    video 151
judgement 171

keywords 64–6, 120
Koch, David 16

Lacy, Sarah 148–50
libraries 40–1; virtual 41–2
listening 16, 85, 93, 115, 121, 127
'living treasures' 44
Lobsenz, Norman 55–6, 108–9
Lyneham, Paul 97–9

managed events 8
Maori 66, 77
Masters, Chris 186, 188–9
media conferences 4, 8

Media Entertainment and Arts Alliance (MEAA) 181
media minder 69–70
Mikac,Walter 182–4
misquoting 161, 167–8
Morrison, Al 127, 132, 137–8, 150
Muldoon, Sir Robert 147
Munro O'Brien, Jodie 6–7, 20–30 *passim*; Iraq 22–9
Murdoch, Rupert 91–2, 106

name dropping 78
National Union of Journalists (NUJ) 181, 187
negotiation 174
nervousness 81–2, 143
new media 49
news interviews 63–4, 110, 117–24, 139–40, 140–7 *passim*, 179
notepads 58–61, 111, 113, 118
notes 60, 63, 111, 116, 118, 123, 157

Oakes, Laurie 62
Obama, President Barack 133, 140–2
objective 13, 15, 78
O'Brien, Kerry 10–11, 14, 17–18, 74–5, 85–6, 95, 97, 110, 122, 128–9, 138–9, 167
observations 120–1
off the record 171, 173, 185
online: content 48; discussions 47; environment 131; information 49; interviewing 160; news sites 39; resources 41–2
open questions 88–9, 141, 145
opinion 3
organising 66–7, 120, 159–60

Pacific Island communities 76, 77
Parkinson, Sir Michael 16–7
Pearson, Mark 181, 190–1
Pedre, Carel 4, 45–6, 129
phone phobia 56
Pilger, John 65
Podcast Network, The (TPN) 131–2
podcasting 132
politeness 74, 155
politicians 5, 11, 12, 44, 94, 155, 172
powers of observation 78–9
Poynter Institute 36, 49
preparation 14, 16, 36, 56
print interviews 108–24 *passim*
privacy 176, 180–2
projection 100–1
pronunciation 150
public relations practitioners 34, 69–71

questions 85–7: and answers 2, 133, 136; avoiding 34; challenge 90, 116; clarification 94; closed 87–8; comment 111, 114; devil's advocate 96, 103; double-barrelled 104; easy 114, 122; embarrassing 34; essential 67, 88; hard 34, 56, 97; 'how does it feel?' 99–100; hypothetical 96; icebreaker 113, 120; informed 86; innocent 101–2; investigative 90–1; leading 102–3; 'must ask' 90; off-beat 122; open 88–9, 145; opening 144–5; opinion 111, 114; organising 120; repeating 94–5; rephrasing 94–5; short 89–90; simple 156–7;'tell me about yourself' 105; tough 15, 103, 116, 156, 158; trick 103; 'who cares' 87, 94, 111, 115; Who, What,

When, Where, Why and How 34, 61, 111, 114; writing down 112
quotes 61, 67, 117, 120, 122, 123, 164–70 *passim*

radio 59–60, 89, 127–8
rapport 73, 76, 80, 120, 135–6
recording devices 58–60, 75, 113, 130; Smartpen 163; 'voice activated' 60
religions 62
repeating 93–5
reputation 189–92
research 119; icebreakers 77–8; investigative journalism 51–2, 109, 186; patterns 34; reasons for 33–5, 146; relationships 34; time for 35–6, 112; trends 34
researchers 44–5
respect 17
Rich, Carole 156–7, 158
rounds 7–9
Ryan, Meg 16

satellite interviews 18–9
scoop 8–9
scrapbooks 40
sensationalism 186
shorthand notes 58, 167
show and tell 174–5
silence 17, 150, 154
Simons, Margaret 131–2
Skype 4, 45–6; conference calls 130; face-to-face interview 133; Instant Messaging (IM) 130; interviews 18–19
social media 45–7
Society of Professional Journalists (SPJ) 181, 187

soft news 3, 4, 14, 109, 117, 140–7
sound 128, 134, 151
sound bites 2, 154
sources 5, 8, 11–13
Spalding, Sally 33, 38–9
spin doctors 70, 71
spontaneous events 8, 9,14
sports stars 12, 119, 155
Stefanovic, Karl 1
street surveys 4
summaries 92–3, 94
Sumpter, Randy 71
surroundings 80, 113, 120–1
swearing 171

talking heads 11
Tankard, James 71
techniques 14–18
technology 18–19, 130
telephone: conversations 175–6; interviews 4–7, 18, 133, 153–7 phone phobia 56
time 128–30
time judgement 145
time-wasting 76
Torres Strait Islanders 62, *passim* 77
trends 34
Trow, Richard 158–9
Twitter 45–7; Twitpic 45, 47

Urban, Andrew 15, 18, 79–81

victims 3, 44, 67, 137, 181, 183–5
videojournalism 151
Voice over Internet Protocol (VoIP) 130

voicers 132, 133–4
vox pops 4

Wendt, Jana 91–2, 106
Winfrey, Oprah 140–2
witnesses 35, 37, 56, 67, 133, 189;
    chequebook journalism 189
Woods, Tiger 8; courtesy 75; news
    angle 64

Woodward, Bob 172
wraps 132, 134

YouTube 46–8

Zuckerberg, Mark 148–50